The Marquesan Journal of Donna Merwick Dening

December 1974-January 1975

With Photographs by Greg Dening

Edited by
Ron Adam

With a Foreword by
Joy Damousi

History Matters No.4

Connor Court Publishing

CONNOR COURT PUBLISHING PTY LTD
PO Box 7257
Redland Bay QLD 4165
sales@connorcourt.com
www.connorcourt.com

Front cover: Photo of Donna on Raiatea by Greg Dening

Maps of Society Islands and Marquesas Islands featuring in the Journal drawn by Adis Elias Fejzić.

Photographs Greg Dening

ISBN: 978-1-925826-81-4 (pbk.)

Cover design by Maria Giordano

Printed in Australia

History Matters Series

Other Volumes:

No.1
THE RED RUGS OF TARSUS
A WOMAN'S RECORD OF THE ARMENIAN
MASSACRE OF 1909
Helen Davenport Gibbons

No.2
WITH THE TURKS IN PALESTINE
Alexander Aaronsohn
Edited by Robert Pascoe

No.3
MEMOIRS OF THE FOURTH CRUSADE AND
THE CONQUEST OF CONSTANTINOPLE
Geoffrey de Villehardouin

HISTORY MATTERS SERIES

It is part of the human condition to make sense of the present as past as soon as it is gone, to tell stories about it and to interpret it. Historians take the process further. They re-present or remake those stories and interpretations in ways that we recognize as 'History'. Historians also have their own interpretations of the past that they find documented in the 'primary sources' – the letters and diaries, the newspaper accounts, the ledgers, committee minutes and parliamentary records, as well as oral testimony – which is why there is always room for contesting how the past is understood and represented.

It is also perhaps part of the human condition to privilege certain interpretations over others and if they do not accord with accepted and prevailing interpretations of 'what actually happened' some historians' views will be discounted. Documents will be overlooked, viewpoints ignored and past voices muted because they do not fit in with mainstream understandings of the past.

The 'History Matters' series is dedicated to publishing histories outside the mainstream. Our acceptance protocols are as strict as other publishers'. But we want to provide an outlet for a wider range of representations of the past by publishing well-researched histories that may be contentious and unconventional, but which nonetheless reflect the diversity and ambiguity of what actually happened in the past. This is important because history matters.

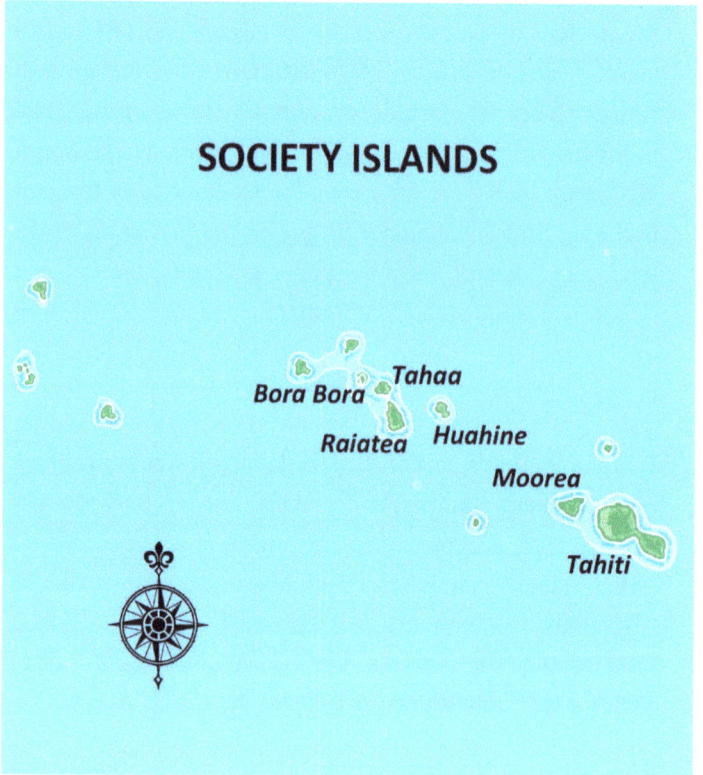

SOCIETY ISLANDS

Tahaa
Bora Bora
Raiatea   Huahine

Moorea

Tahiti

Society Islands referred to in the Journal

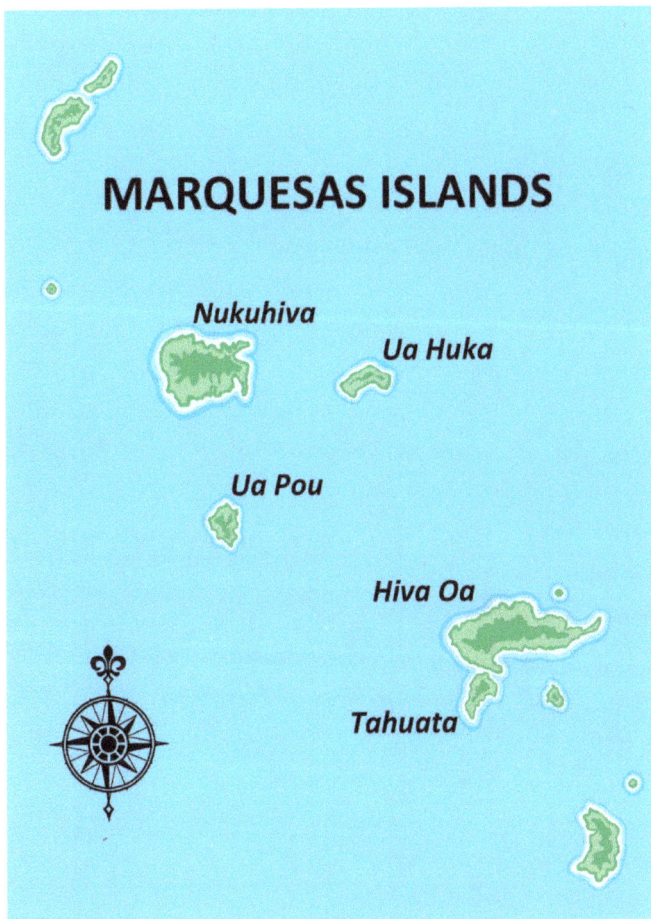

MARQUESAS ISLANDS

Nukuhiva

Ua Huka

Ua Pou

Hiva Oa

Tahuata

Marquesas Islands referred to in the Journal

I dedicate this publication to Greg

and the Marquesan people.

FOREWORD

Donna Merwick was born in 1932, in Chicago, Illinois, USA. Donna studied history at Mundelein College – a Catholic liberal Arts college in Chicago – prior to joining the Order of the Sisters of Charity of the Blessed Virgin Mary in 1953. In 1962, she completed her MA at DePaul University and then her PhD at the University of Wisconsin, Madison in 1967. In 1966, she began teaching history at Mundelein College; two years later, in 1968, she left the Order.*

In 1969, Donna arrived as a Lecturer in History at the University of Melbourne. In the 26 years that followed, and until her retirement in 1995, Donna taught American history. Building on a life-long interest in theories of history and philosophical understandings of historical practice and method, she also taught the honours seminar, the Philosophy of History in the Twentieth Century.** In doing so, Donna inspired and influenced generations of students in new approaches to studying and writing history. In 1971, she married Greg Dening, the leader of the so called 'Melbourne School', which promoted ethnographic history, drawing together insights from the intersections between history and anthropology. Together with Rhys Isaac and Inga Clendinnen, Donna and Greg were pioneers in this approach in charting the impact of cultural and social change across time and place.

Donna's first monograph – based on her PhD dissertation from the University of Wisconsin – was *Boston Priests, 1848-1910: A Study of Social and Intellectual Change* (Harvard University Press, 1973) where Donna explored three generations of nineteenth century Boston priests to examine the opposition to Irish Catholicism in Boston. In a study of social and cultural change, *Boston Priests* provides new and innovative insights of the changing nature of Boston Catholicism.

Donna's research interests shifted from this focus to the seventeenth century and, in particular, to the Dutch in New York. Publications between 1990 and 2013 cemented her reputation as a pioneering and leading scholar, one of the most distinguished, significant and influential historians of Dutch New York. *Possessing Albany, 1630-1710: The Dutch and English Experiences* (Cambridge University Press, 1990) explored how the Dutch in seventeenth century New York 'possessed' the new world. Exploring cultural change through narratives, stories and maps employed by the Dutch to define and give meaning to the landscapes they were transforming, *Possessing Albany* marked a clear shift from social to cultural history through the deployment of post-modern narratives and approaches.

The publication of the classic and path-breaking *Death of a Notary: Conquest and Change in Colonial New York* (Columbia University Press, 1999) further established Donna as one of the most significant historians of her generation. Focusing on the suicide of the Dutch notary of Albany Adriaen Janse van IIpendam, in 1686, *Death of a Notary* brilliantly and compellingly recreates a dramatically changing world when the British take over the colony. Janse van IIpendam's world is overturned when New Netherland became New York. The shifts of this cataclysmic shift are traced at the everyday level with meticulous attention to detail and a remarkable reconstruction from the historical sources. The book remains a pioneering work for the deft use of microhistory to transform our understanding of the dramatic and enduring impact of social and cultural change. It is a master class in the historian's craft.

Death of a Notary was followed in 2006 with *The Shame and the Sorrow: Dutch-Amerindian Encounters in New Netherland* (University of Pennsylvania Press). Continuing the theme of cultural change and conquest, *The Shame and the Sorrow* explores the violent encounter of the Dutch and the native peoples following the West India Company's purchase of Manhattan Island in 1625. In a challenging and provocative engagement with this encounter, Donna assesses how to judge the Dutch in the destruction of the native cultures. She argues that it was not the intention of the Dutch to embark on conquest and violence, initially seeking to develop colonial commerce with native peoples. But this did not turn out to be the case. What transpired was a brutal and murderous attack on the Indian settlement at Pavonia, destroying the native population in the lower Hudson Valley. Donna's concern is the way the Dutch participated in these massacres and how this violence undermined their values and ideals and led to much examination and introspective blaming within the Dutch community.

The career of Peter Stuyvesant, New Netherland's last and longest serving director, forms the subject of Donna's latest book, *Stuyvesant Bound: An Essay on Loss Across Time* (University of Pennsylvania Press, 2013). The winner of the Hendricks award in 2015 from the New Netherlands Institute for the best book on New Netherland and the Dutch colonial experience, *Stuyvesant Bound* is the study of Stuyvesant, who governed the colony for 17 years. Donna arranges the study along the themes of loss, which are explored on multiple levels – including the loss of his career and the colony. More broadly, Donna makes a wider point. A further loss, she argues, involves that of the comprehension and understanding of emotions and reasoning of seventeenth century Dutchmen when historians read Stuyvesant through hindsight and with a teleological lens. The analysis and reading of Stuyvesant's life that Donna advances in this work focuses on the limits of the times in which Stuyvesant lived, such as his duty, his faith and encounters with loss throughout his life and career.

Across her stellar and distinguished career, Donna has recast our understandings of the seventeenth century Dutch colony of New Netherland, recreating its society with narratives which are nuanced, subtle, powerful and compelling. Highly original, innovative, challenging, evocative and transformative, her works have set the highest bar in scholarly excellence, skilfully providing new interpretations through the art of historical storytelling.

Joy Damousi
Professor of History, University of Melbourne
6th January 2020

---

*   Susan Foley and Charles Sowerwine, Donna Jeane Merwick (1932–), The Encyclopedia of Women and Leadership in twentieth-century Australia, http://www.womenaustralia.info/leaders/biogs/WLE0421b.htm

** David Goodman and Mike McDonnell, 'An interview with Donna Merwick', *Australasian Journal of American Studies*, vol.34, no.1, July 2015, p.60.

EDITOR'S PREFACE

The voyage on which you are about to vicariously embark begins in mid-December 1974 in Tahiti, where Donna Merwick Dening and her husband Greg Dening lived on the outskirts of the capital Papeete with locals Aritana and Victorine Hozolet. The voyage takes in the other Society Islands to the east, Moorea, Huahine, Raiatea and Tahaa, before taking us west to the journey's ultimate destination – the Marquesan islands. With their ancient maraes falling into disrepair, their lonely graves neglected, and their monuments to European dreams deteriorating, the Society Islands anticipated what was to come in the Marquesas. Anticipated but did not fully prepare Donna and Greg for the experiences that awaited them at the end of December 1974 and the beginning of January 1975 on the islands of Hiva Oa, Tahuatu, Ua Huka, Nukuhiva and Ua Pou. In the Marquesas, Greg later reflected, the silence of the land enveloped them both and made them conscious of being intruders.

Donna had two purposes in keeping a journal. She signals them in the opening sentence of her first entry, penned just before she and Greg disembarked at Tahiti. 'If I want to write this like a novel, gracefully', she writes, 'I want to begin with Greg.' Greg had been appointed in 1971 Max Crawford Professor of History at his alma mater, the University of Melbourne, where Donna was also a recent appointment. Both had established reputations as fine historians. Donna for her 1973 publication *Boston Priests, 1848-1910: A Study of Social and Intellectual Change*, and Greg for *The Marquesan Journal of Edward Robarts* (1974) together with his paradigm-shifting articles on the Pacific and on the sociology of knowledge, especially historical knowledge. For both, their best known history writing was ahead of them; in Donna's journal we gain a taste of the flavor of what was to come.

For Donna, the voyage to Tahiti and the Marquesas was an opportunity to experiment with a more adventurous and unorthodox form of writing history – 'like a novel, 'gracefully', as she says in her opening journal entry. Her journal, then, might be read as a precursor for the kind of transformative writing style that characterized her later award-winning histories – *Possessing Albany, 1630-1710: The Dutch and English Experiences* (1990), *Death of a Notary: Conquest and Change in Colonial New York* (1999), *The Shame and the Sorrow: Dutch-Amerindian Encounters in New Netherland* (2006), and *Stuyvesant Bound: An Essay on Loss Across Time* (2013).

Keeping a journal was also an opportunity for Donna to record her affection and admiration as well as sense of responsibility for Greg. The first entry, for 11 December 1974, records how being with Greg holds her 'excited & so happy', how the hours are 'luminous … with Greg looking young and suntanned', how he buys her chocolates and beams to see her in her straw hat. 'I am still not able to connect beauty (Beauty) with a God' she writes, 'only Greg'. The journal's final entry, for 6 January 1975, closes with: 'Greg bought me French perfume; has a headache. So good to me.' Here and in other entries throughout the journal we catch a glimpse of the style of her later award-winning books, with transcendent themes traced out with descriptions of the everyday.

After reading the transcript of the journal, a relative remarked: 'It reads like a love letter to Greg'. Indeed it does. And making the journal available to a wider audience was always going to carry the risk of Donna being seen as just an adjunct to Greg and his work. That would be a serious misreading of their relationship. And it would ignore the experiential reality that underpinning and sustaining any individual act of writing is the social relational context in which the writing occurs. At the end of her Preface written in August 2018 Donna remarks that it never occurred to her that she might have used her time in the Marquesas as a basis for research of her own. 'I did, however, know quite clearly that my companionship for Greg was essential to him and perhaps for his work. He needed it and was grateful'. And that, she adds, was enough. The reciprocity of their love, in which giving features as much, at times more, than receiving, comes across clearly in the journal, which makes it an important biographical document for two of the most important historians of the last half century.

The journal is also important in terms of Donna's experimenting with writing narrative 'like a novel.

An experiment by someone on the way to becoming the acclaimed writer that Joy Damousi celebrates in her Foreword. An experiment by someone who, in accepting responsibility as an historian for how she represented those about whom she writes, contributed powerfully to the reflexive turn that characterized the so-called Melbourne School of History in which she was a leading figure.

For Greg, the voyage was an opportunity – his only opportunity – to experience what it meant to set foot in the Marquesas, which until then he had known only 'through the texts that innumerable intruders into this vast ocean had made of their experiences." (*Beach Crossings: Voyaging Across Times, Cultures and Self*, 2004, p. 57). One of those texts was *The Marquesan Journal of Edward Robarts*, which Greg had transcribed and edited in time for him to bring copies with him to the Marquesas in 1974. The 'pride of my academic life to this time', he later wrote (*Beach Crossings* p. 58). Being in the Marquesas enabled him not only, as he later reflected, to 'put spatial images' to his stories (p.78), but to fundamentally recast those stories. Meeting the old Marquesan man Teifitu at Atuona on Hiva Oa the day after Christmas 1974, he tells us, made him decide to write *Islands and Beaches: Discourse on a Silent Land – Marquesas 1774-1880* (1980) the way he did. The meeting would not have been the same, in all probability would never have happened, but for Donna, to whom Greg dedicated *Islands and Beaches*, 'for the islands we have made and the beaches we have crossed'. In the Acknowledgements he pays tribute to how Donna 'shared all the hard days of research and writing and made the good days better with her encouragement and support'. The good days – as well as the bad – are recorded in the journal.

Without Donna, Greg would have been profoundly isolated in the Marquesas. In 'Remarks on a Silent Land' at the end of *Islands and Beaches,* he expresses the regret that he never came to know the living Marquesans as he knew the dead. 'I have this half-suspicion', he confesses, that Aoe, outsiders like himself, 'bring their silence with them.' In Teifitu he found a soul mate, an 'old man ... not made for fibreglass boats, for commerce or for the vigour of new authority. Politicking had passed him by, and there was no market for the sort of knowledge he possessed.' With Teifitu he walked deep into the valleys of Tahuata and talked about the past, the wanton killings and passing of the old order, and Donna's journal records how he wept at the old man's descriptions. But apart from Teifitu there was no other Marquesan with whom Greg established such a meaningful relationship. Like the old man, Greg himself was not made for fibreglass boats, for commerce or for the vigour of new authority, and there was no market among the other Marquesan men for the sort of knowledge he possessed. It was different for Donna. She was accepted into a circle of local women, and through them their children and their domestic sphere. While Greg could not be part of the women's world, through Donna he was able to embrace the human connection it afforded. As Donna's Preface, accurately I think, reflects, Greg needed her companionship, without which he could not have made the islands and crossed the beaches in quite the same way.

Donna has captured the everyday actions and interactions that constituted this companionship, so that the journal provides unique firsthand insights into otherwise unknown aspects of researching and envisaging *Islands and Beaches*. Greg documented some of the process himself in *Beach Crossings*, where he reflects back on his brief time in Fenua'enata ('The Land', the Marquesas) three decades earlier. 'Being there', he writes, meant 'making a voyage to those places where the past is imprinted on the landscape. It is touching, feeling, smelling, hearing the past there, having the silence envelop one, crossing the beach and being conscious of one's intrusion' (p.55). And in Donna's journal we find descriptions of what it meant at the everyday experiential level to touch and feel and smell and hear that past. The journal provides depth and nuance to the experience. In its frank and disarming honesty it captures the anxieties and fears, the frustrations and disappointments, as well as the rewards and accomplishments that were part of the voyage to The Land.

These are captured with an astute eye and a penetrating candor at times giving way to an uneasiness that perhaps only an account not written for a wider audience can give. And this is precisely why the journal warrants a wider audience. As Greg notes in the Preface to *Islands and Beaches*:

'Essays on method should first begin with a diary of research. Diaries would catch with more honesty the bleak days, the chance discoveries, the opportunistic sallies, the fumbling questions and the occasional rewarding days of light and excitement when understanding or new knowledge rewards the effort it takes to uncover one tiny corner of the universe of truth. I have not written such a diary' (p. 4) But, fortunately for us, Donna has.

Just as Donna catches the bleak days and chance discoveries in her journal, so too does Greg in the photographs he took. There are a couple of hundred of them, retrieved from miscellaneous cardboard boxes and metal slide carousels in the backyard study when their home was put up for sale some years after Greg's death in 2008. Greg had started equipping himself for the role of photographer before leaving Melbourne, with mixed results. As he notes in *Beach Crossings* (p.58), he had 'failed rather badly' in the photography classes he had taken in preparation for his visit to the Fenua'enata. He had been too timid to enter the private space of those 'interesting' faces of the poor and old and eccentric his teachers wanted him to invade. The timidity returned in the Society Islands and the Marquesas, for which there are very few photographs of people. Rather, the focus is on the sea and the mountains, the derelict maraes. This was not only less invasive but also in keeping with the theme of a silent past imprinted on the landscape. Given that Greg set out to write a discourse on a silent land, the photographs might be viewed as a visual record of what 'being there' in that silent land meant.

For the journal's publication we, Donna and I, selected a couple of dozen photographs from the hundreds that Greg took in December 1974 and January 1975. Nearly all were taken by him. A few – when Greg is the subject – were shot by Donna. Very occasionally a third person used Greg's camera to take a photo of them together. Most of the photographs are testimony to Greg's repeated attempts to capture the mood of the sea and the landscape and to document the deteriorating artefacts of ancient Polynesian cultures. Fewer than one in twenty are of the people with whom they came into contact: people like Aritana and Victorine Holozet in Tahiti, and in the Marquesas the old man Teifitu and Marie-Ange and the other women and the children who welcomed the visitors and rewarded them with their smiles and dances. The captions are as Greg wrote them on the slide mounts.

The slides and the original journal are housed in the Pacific Collection, University of Hawai'i-Manoa Library, where they are available for reference. It is Donna's hope that an exhibition of the Marquesan photographs will be held sometime in the future at Te Ana Peua, the Tahuata Museum dedicated to rediscovering, celebrating and protecting Marquesan culture.

Ron Adams
7th January 2020

NOTE ON TRANSCRIPTION

Transcribing the journal was not altogether straightforward. Written nearly half a century ago on sixty 9 x 15cm ruled notepad pages, the handwriting is neat but tiny. Some of the entries were written in red ink. Sometimes text was added after the original entry, and at other times gaps were left to accommodate further detail or reflections that were never added. It was difficult and a couple of times impossible to decipher some words, even with Donna's help. Three people helped reduce the impossible words down to a mere handful: my colleague Lesley Birch drew upon her past experience making sense of doctors' notes; another colleague, Megan Garratt, used detective skills honed through trying to make her way out of Escape Rooms; and my wife Robyn Adams tapped into her school teacher acumen to identify words through context rather than the script.

It fell to me to decide on what to do with the occasional misspelling, obvious slip, or inconsistency. Correct them for ease of reading and to accord with the writer's intended meaning? Or reproduce them to be faithful to what was actually written? After careful consideration and discussions with Donna on the pros and cons, I opted for the latter, adding corrections in square brackets immediately after the offending word. In the case of some words – like 'magasin', which is rendered as both 'magasin' and 'magazin' throughout the journal, or 'marae', which is also spelt 'maree' – I have retained the original spelling with the correction added in square brackets only after the first misspelling. Polynesian place names are reproduced as they were – phonetically – written, followed by the accepted standard spelling in square brackets for the initial reference.

Obvious slips, such as wrong choice of word, have been retained, followed by a question mark in square brackets [?]. Question marks in round brackets (?) are part of the original text.

One of the reasons for publishing the journal is to throw further light on the relationship between what Greg Dening experienced in the Marquesas and his later representations of the experience. To this end, endnotes cross reference information in the journal with what was published in *Islands and Beaches: Discourse on a Silent Land – Marquesas 1774-1880* (University Press of Hawaii, 1980*)* and *Beach Crossings: Voyaging Across Times, Cultures and Self* (Melbourne University Publishing, 2004). This has also enabled comparisons between Donna's and Greg's perspectives on events and people. The other publication used for cross-referencing is Patrick O'Reilly's *Tahitiens: Répertoire Bibiographique de la Polynésie Française* (Musée de l'Homme, 1975), for information of individuals mentioned in the journal.

PREFACE

Life is a Beach

Almost fifty years have passed since I wrote the journal you are about to read. Once finished, I gave it residence in my typical historian's study. There it occupied a space with hundreds of other documents: drafts of chapters of books, articles in learned journals, student submissions, reports, reviews of colleagues' work, copies of correspondence, committee reports, agendas and minutes. Each of these somehow found housing in file drawers, a computer's desktop, on overloaded shelving brought in from Ikea. Even the arrival of the print eWorld only seemed to double the 'stuff', endangering the certain whereabouts of each bit of it. Much was sure to get displaced. More likely, lost.

For most of the years, the journal lay in a shallow desk drawer. The small, black leather notebook demanded little space, and less attention. It could easily seem of no importance. The accompanying slides (later digitalized) were in another room. They cluttered a black box made to hold 3" by 5" file cards.

Why did they not – one or the other of them – get lost? Why did I save them?

In recent years, I had heard rumours of a (highly unlikely) museum or library having been established at Nukuhiva in the Marquesas. I considered the possibility that a curator might accept the journal and slides. Didn't I have an obligation to play my small part in contributing to the history of these people? A responsibility to pass on the photos we took of the children whom you'll briefly meet? They would now be in their sixties or seventies. Would they still be in the Marquesas? Or living in Papeete in Tahiti? The port city was, after all, an alluring place of lights and constant movement. The 'big smoke' to the children. It meant a ticket to a job, an opening to travel, maybe ownership of a motorbike.

Writing this reflection, I can retrospectively gauge how I made selection of the experiences that I would describe in its pages. I realize now that emotions acted as a dividing line separating experiences that went undescribed, because I could manage them reasonably well, from experiences where fear dominated and writing was perhaps the only way I could cope with the high level of anxiety evident in its pages. So, to consider the first, there were moments when I felt myself to be in familiar circumstances. For example, I felt a belonging in the simple New England-type Catholic church. I recognized the hymns, the order of the Mass liturgy, the orderly distribution of the children in the pews: girls to one side of the main aisle, boys to the other. I registered quickly to the supervisory demeanor of the Sisters. I warmed to the carefully carved native statue of the Virgin Mary at the front of the church, which seemed to have been given pride of place and stood as testimony to the parish priest Mgr Le Cléac'h's determination to decolonialize the precinct of the Church on the island as much as possible.

But it's descriptions aroused by uncertainty or worry or fear that take up a disproportionate presence in the journal. So, it gives no detailed description of our house in Nukuhiva. Only caught in the narrative are the rats scratching their foul way along the thatched roofing of the ceiling. It gives little space to the panoramic views of the island's topography. Just a sense of how the mountainous peaks and ravines had done nothing to welcome us. No fond adieu as we made our return journey to the airstrip. Instead, the journal registers my anxiety in a jeep driven (as I thought) much too close to the edge of the twisting dirt road. The anxiety deepened when conversation turned to the departure of the plane: pity that it had got double-booked. I described all that.

But nothing on how, arriving at the airstrip, we were efficiently boarded. The flight to an over-night stop in Tahiti and then on to Honolulu also went unrecorded – probably because there was no fear: I was leaving the Marquesas Islands. And I never returned.

***

I'd left behind what scholars would call the existential experiences of a cross-cultural encounter. My subsequent years were to be spent theorizing and writing historical narratives about the lives of those who had, for one reason or another, undertaken to make the dislocating, often hazardous, and sometimes regretted crossing of the sea from their own reasonably manageable safe, familiar cultures to an unknown other.

Those studies helped me realize that I had not prepared myself well enough for the cost of crossing into the Marquesan people's realities. As a result, I remained the outsider. I found myself too quickly querying their apparent lack of inclusiveness, the limits they put on trust and openness, their guarded sociability. The women accepted me as a species, a sort of outsider but benign. They marvelled that I must be very rich to travel as far as their islands – while they were housebound, spending the days making poi from breadfruit. I came to conclude, however, that the men – with whom I seldom had a lengthy (comfortable) encounter – would never let me be anything other than an outsider. Like the unwelcoming pervasive geography of mountain ridges and deep valleys, they were agents of exclusion. My outsiderness was a consequence of their exclusionary temperament. Nothing of my doing.

***

The Manoa campus of the University of Hawaii is remarkably close to Waikiki beach. A short bus ride connects the university to Kuhio, an avenue that parallels Kalakalua, which in turn runs along Waikiki beach. Some years after composing the journal you are about to read, there appeared on Waikiki and the adjacent streets a joyful T-shirt message: 'Life Is A Beach.' Greg made the *beach* famous as a metaphor for a liminal space, that in-between space that separates the culture that an individual has left behind from the not-yet-achieved enculturation in a new milieu. The four words on the T-shirt were enough to signify all the surrounding pleasures and fun of leave-vacationing – from college obligations, office work, daily forms of household drudgery. Near the surf at Waikiki, the metaphor worked when it had returning home to anticipate but, for a limited time, set aside. Or in the carnivalesque revelry of Shrove Tuesday, where the purpose of its celebration is to prepare for the rigors, denials and abstinences of Lent. Or in a honeymoon, where the point is to have extravagant fun before settling into married life.

***

Returning to the Marquesan story. I came to realize that, unlike my own lack of preparation to cross the beach, in France my friend Mgr Le Cléac'h would undoubtedly have prepared diligently for the years ahead in the forbidding, strange, challenging islands of the central Pacific where he was to be missioned. Perhaps he made a Retreat in order to embed the ways of prayer and peace that might fortify him for the rugged years – maybe a lifetime – ahead.

My days and weeks in the Marquesas had received no such preparation. And, while there, I did not anticipate that they might have had value for some on-going or future research. I did, however, know quite clearly that my companionship for Greg was essential to him and perhaps for his work. He needed it and was grateful.

And that was enough.

Donna Merwick Dening
10th August 2018

JOURNAL

December 11, 1974

If I want to write this like a novel, gracefully, I want to begin with Greg. Just now – and I am writing narrative – he printed my name on the permit to disembark at Tahiti: careful, rounded letters & numbers, like a bank clerk's. I am too tired to think exactly, carefully of all that holds me excited & so happy. The past hours were luminous for me, with Greg looking young & suntanned, quiet and waiting for whatever will come, like me. He bought me lime chocolat[e]s & beamed to see me in my straw hat. I am still not able to connect beauty (Beauty) with a God, only Greg. Dinner at the pier was Sydney at its lov[e]liest – I feel divine.

December 10-14

We are living with Victorine & Aritana Hozolet [Holozet]¹ in their house at Faaa (fouboug of Papeete). A very modest house, at least the surrounds are indicative of a settled, simple "commune", as it is called. The house is reached by turning left off the maisons & vaguely, discomfortingly tawdry mainroad from Papeete out to Puanuia [Puna'auia][2] & around the island. At the turn to Holozets' house is a double-storey, old, latticed & half-abandoned S. Maugham-like house; some carelessly-dressed & poor Tahitians sweep the corner of the road there & seem to have no purpose (or need) other than to wait for the bus which comes to a jerking, tumultuous stop there. The small __rue__ to Holozet is dirt, lined with red-leafed shrubs; not dark but depressingly rather than lushly green & overgrown. A new house is being built on the right, 100 yds beyond the empty, staring double-storey house. It is largely cement blocks, very slowly laid & daily forming the shape of a house.

'Aritana Vict[orine] Anthrop[ologist]'

What of Aritana et Victorine? Their house, in the "commune" has maximum privacy, surrounded by an (to Western ways) over-grown garden: tiare de Tahiti, coconut, mango; Victorine has nurtured many orchids and "jack in the pulpit". 7 dogs (all are cousins, descendants, whether human or les chiens: these are of the family of 2 fierce dogs up the mountains behind Papeete (Faaa) & guarding the home of Victorine's sister. So: 7 dogs which bark on our arrival – or that of strangers. Remember most? large coffee cups w/o handles (NOT seen at Maeva Beach or L'Auberge de Pacifique), fog lights, white biscuits & jam (shortage of sucre) for breakfast & marvelous coffee served in a thermos; American household goods: Lux soap, the smell of over-ripe mango and plumeria mixed with more than occasional odours of something rotting.

'Tahiti: Matavai Back Mountains'

December 16th

We toured the island with Aritana. Met Peter Van Cam of Marquesas. He immediately offered us pear liqueur from Switzerland. A heavy man, his father was a political man, deported to Tahiti in the 1890's (?), then to the Marquesas.[3] 2 rooms: a primitive painting of the nearby cascade. We spoke easily, he is a "wise man", educated in Marquesas to 8 years. At "Marquesas" he made signals like lifting one's arm.

We stopped at A's cousins all along the way. In the rain, entered under a large garage, ran to a house, *entering the lower floor of 1 room where A. found rum & made a drink. Upstairs, the house was mostly a large balcony, with hibiscus on the railing & 2 very large & relatively empty bedrooms. All cousins & relatives may stay there. As elsewhere, A. <u>uses</u> the land; his sister Sophie owns ½ the land.*

We saw the anchorage of Cook; a decayed, forgotten "monument" to the first Spanish priests was discovered near a dilapidated home. It was nearly hidden by a decaying banana tree, the cross also missing.

'Tahiti: Marae Arahurahu'

'Tahiti: Sunset'

December 18

Reflections

The poor are unrestricted – from the domination of space (not enough clothes-hangers, not enough space for clothes to air, dry – simplicity comes to have to wear wrinkled clothes, small bugs in coffee, flies on slices of pineapple, the same damp tablecloth ...

Syrup mango; cooled roof, incense-like smell of Chinese (Hong Kong) wares; greasy smells & rotting fruit; children w. rat; children at Raiatea airport playing on the steps for the plane passengers;[4]

December 18

Went around Moorea. Hired a jeep; Greg said, for the driving, he felt like a German general, but it was more like difficult fieldwork, i.e. rutted roads, rain, coconut groves w. rotting husks. Stopped to photograph Cook Bay from the Arnica (?) Hotel; very shallow bay (?), very green; no respectable villages anywhere. The rain closed in on us after Onupoiohu [Opunohu] Bay, so high conical & finger-shaped mountains were invisible, sadly. Aritana, along the way, (ah, marees [maraes] [along the] coast in terrible disrepair & rain prevented us going to the inland maree repaired by Bishop Museum) stopped an elderly fisherman coming in with a young girl & young man in a light blue wooden canoe, & cajoled him to give 4 fish, very dark brown &, to me, unattractive. He threw them unceremoniously into a raincoat he spread out & we continued, <u>after</u> A. got the bewildered man's name – to send him "a picture".

'Moorea: Opunohu'

The tour took us between rows of ramshackled pink, blue, aquamarine houses, all surrounded now by pools of whitish water. Abandoned churches with sadly neglected graves that seemed to beg for attention to the sacrifice made on this – as it looked to me – God-forsaken island. We could not get many photographs but, without sullenness, returned to Elizabeth's, i.e. A's cousin's magasin. There we ate the fish – nearly raw & tasteless (holding the fish, my fingers kept digging into his eye, but I found myself not caring, <u>enjoying</u> the experience of picking at the brown fish). Before eating, we were served – whisky

& water each; Elizabeth watched from the window of the magazin [magasin]. We then had a large bottle of cheap red wine & ice – delicious & we fell to talking of children, family, Greg & all of us much enjoying it. After returning to the airport, we reached Papeete in the rain.

'Tahiti: Tahara'a and Pupotea'

In the evening, we ate at a School Hall recommended by Victorine. The self-service was simple & those eating were young people, well behaved – began to feel like a Salvation Army temple. We met Dana Getzhek (?), her brother Casey & their father. Together with her sister & C's friend, they'd sailed in "Tradition" from San Diego; they'd seen the Marquesas, anchoring off Hiva Oa, etc. We were pleased to get further information. With Dana, we watched a Christmas "speech night" – young boys & then 'teen aged girls doing traditional dance. The folk seemed happy to share their music – & sandwiches – with us. Home at 9:30.[5]

December 19: Raiatea

Rose at 7:00 to have our usual breakfast at A's: coffee in green glass cups & from the thermos, as well as fresh pineapple slices. Talked with A. of his school-teachers' meeting. He took us to the airport where we took off in a steamy, stuffy plane of 20 passengers. (We took (me greedily) candies, for later.) Greg took photos from the plane of Tahiti's coast, than Moorea, getting Le Baie de Cook before cloud covered the view. The photos of Huahine, very beautiful & almost bisected by lagoon & bays. We landed there affording pictures of the reefs. Raiatea was 10 min. away, & nearby Tahaa. Both had strong sunshine when we arrived. We have a bungalow, # 2, &, shortly, toured the island in a neglected yellow VW. Greg got only a few pictures along the dirt road to Opoa, for the afternoon rain closed in. But at Opoa, we were able *to photograph the great maree along the sea, very impressive as it was not restored. Returning, the sun appeared sufficiently for us to photograph Faaroa Bay – the lovliest we've seen thus far. Mountains, rising 800 & 900 ft., jutted up immediately from the road around the bay. They were, of course, the edges of the volcano & we had been journeying in the crater. We passed Bali Hai & then the airport, finding it possible to photograph Bora Bora, Tahaa & then a small coastal maree. The maree, <u>directly</u> on the sea, was, partialially [partially] at least, used now as a tip. Local residents (an old lady, in greeting, kissed me) were preparing for Christmas. Children were flying small, white paper kites. We found it difficult to avoid land crabs & chickens along the road.*

'Raiatea: Marae Taputapuatea'

Dinner at Bali Hai, 175 F & very delicious. Lime/ vodka beforehand – & popcorn!

December 20: Jonathon's Birthday[6]

Slept wonderfully. Boat trip to Tahaa a slight disappointment, tho' a few pictures. Saw some lovely Tahitian graves in families' gardens. In the afternoon, we read, rowed the outrigger – they afford incredible smoothness. Leave Raiatea at 5:15. Took a plane now more humid & close; Tahitian children took handsful of candies, a bulldog in the mail compartment. Walked to Aritana's & found Victorine alone, preparing to [go to] a fétè at her sister's new house. She urged us to go, just for an hour, as they were invited to dinner at the magistrate's. Aritana was already there & engaging V's many relatives in an oration, as oldest male member of the family. A new & expensive house, the 2nd floor opened on a long balcony which afforded a magnificent view of Papeete Harbour. Along the full length of the balcony were family members & separating two long lines of these were long tables laden with hors d'oeuvres & wine glasses. A happy occasion when, w/o fluent French or even talking, one felt one was accepted & was at ease. We toasted with champagne, then had open sandwich[e]s & cakes, then Victorine brought us her own 4-day brewed Tahitian punch: fruits &

rum. We left at 8:00 & went to the Pizzeria where we ate for the first time in the day. I had fresh tuna in a pizza &, as before, we both had cafe Liegenois [café liegéois]. Tom Jones singing, & The Sting!

December 21

We prepared to leave for the Marquesas tomorrow. Had breakfast with A & V, avocado & good black coffee. Changed money for the islands; enjoyed seeing again the waterfront: "Tradition", the Chinese junk restaurant, a parade of T-shirts (Kick, Tahiti Prison, U. of San Antonio, Texas). Bought books, etc.; had lunch at Tiara, Hinano Beer. Returned in sunshine & visited w. Aritana: tour of his garden. Not "pretty" but plentiful: apple cucumber, mango, lime, onion, 2 pineapple types, 3 banana types, cocoanut, avocado, breadfruit, vanilla, coffee.

'Tahiti: Aritana and Mangoes'

Despite a reservation for four at "Auberge" at 7, A & V were still casually talking on the porch, the TV on but no interest. Heavy rain. We left at 7:45, & A produced leis of flowers for Greg & a "corona" of plumeria for me & Victorine. V's face was a mask but it was clear they were the flowers ordered for friends arriving the next day from New Zealand! Dinner was lovely: V. simply the true Tahitian lady. We ordered Sprite & vodka &, when drinks came w/o limes, A ordered them. V & A used forks to break the skins, as <u>must</u> be done! A wanted it to be a special evening & was overjoyed when a Tahitian began singing to his own guitar accompaniment. A. danced – clearly *(as he explained to me) for us rather than mere exhibitionism. We took our wine – & later creme de cacoa [crème de cacao] – with ice; A. used the small cup some crutons came in to give some of his soup to V. Tremendous kindness – V. enjoying it all but never effusively. $80.00 (U.S)*

December 22

At 7:30 we took off in the rain for Atuona: leis, corona, some baggage left with A & V. By 10 a. m. we had passed many of the Tuamotus; did not land at Rangiroa. Some clear skies but largely driving rain; unable to see. The pilots we found most amusing; one is teaching the other, so each reaches uncertainly for various instruments! We are directly behind the pilots. Stopped to re-fuel (from gasoline drums!) at Manihi, a dreadfully forsaken coral atoll. Gravel[l]y grey coral, immensely hardened, & little vegetation. No toilet, so each went behind the thatched shed that served for an airport! We are now c. 9 passengers, 4 hours to Hiva Oa. At 10:30 we took off; by 10:45 sunshine![7]

'Manihi: Res[earch] Ass[istant]'

And the skies remained beautifully clear, giving a promise of clear skies over Hiva Oa, four hours away. The co-pilot assumed command, & for 45 min, the pilot served as "steward", i.e. unpacking lunch trays in the rear & handing them forward. It was an unexpected – & delicious – surprise, by far the most appreciated & indeed most attractively prepared flight meal we've had. It was accompanied by wines &, of course, mineral water. The lunch as well as the continuous blue skies made the flight from Manihi something so different – & so much more enjoyable – from the previous leg of the journey. Greg, I could tell, felt much better & it all seemed yet another sign *of good days in the Marquesas. The approach to Hiva Oa (I believe we passengers saw the islands <u>before</u> the pilots did) was the most spectacular I've ever seen.*

'Vaitahu: From Air'

Because we were so few continuing on to Hiva Oa, there were empty seats and because the pilots seemed completely occupied in just landing the plane, Greg could move excitedly from a position to photograph Tahuata (& deep blue Vaitahu Bay) & over to photograph Hiva Oa & its enormous mountain heights.[8] Levelling for the landing, the plane found balance & came onto a runway carved out of a plateau & between 2 reaches of mountains.[9] A driving rain had just come up, driving so horizontally that puddles of rainwater were unaffected – or so I thought as I stood in the thatched hut that served for the airport. Some 15 Marquesans waiting & about 4 jeeps, the only type of vehicle in the islands. Mayor Rauzy[10] & his wife collected the pilots & Professor Moser, along with some children. We were taken by a native of France, a large man, a sailor, in his jeep along the 13 k road to Atuona. A very difficult & rutted road, along steep terrain w. noticeably less vibrant or indeed beautiful vegetation than the Society Islands. He said: 5000 Marquesans; friendly acc[ording] to the development of the village (gendarmerie, school, priest etc.); interisland school; valley still cut off from neighboring valley; Dec. best month for fishing for the sea is calm; copra is the only industry.

I found Atuona very unlike my expectation. I'd imagined a small community along a waterfront, perhaps some 2-storey _magasins_, _some_ fishing boats – a rather miniature Papeete. I expected some clutches of activity, _some_ density of buildings, some small evidence of, as it were, looking outward from the sea-side. It is quite different – to my enjoyment of watching people interact & bustle, disappointing. For the sea at Atuona does form a beach, catching the surf & waves of a magnificent bay. But there is no waterfront. Instead the beach, with its black sand, was & remained a deserted beach: no yachts, no copra boat, no wharf. Running at right angles to the latitude of the beach, Atuona is 2 sides of a road, the same one which comes down the mountain from the airport, turns at the beach & leads thru' the village of spaciously set houses (not unlike FAAA but tidier & w. more property).

'Atuona: Mt Temetui from Cemetery'

For us, it meant following the road to 2 bungalows owned by Rauzy, houses & R's restaurant located at the foot of a magnificently high mountain, now standing out against blue skies. We shared the bungalow w Prof. Moser, a Swiss gentleman, <u>en route</u> to teach a semester on international law in Brazil. A walk took us past Marquesans playing bingo but not otherwise congregated together &, it appeared to me, not very friendly. The village had the sense of a dead Sunday afternoon, with the gloom of seriousness. All our while here – & it <u>was</u> short – no merriment, no sound of singing, no jolly friends together. Everything as quiet as the closed general stores. The beach was beautiful, reminiscent of Australia but sadly lacking its jovial, noisy people – we saw no single family together; everything immensely quiet & ordered (in the worst sense). Climbed along the rocks (lava flows quite in evidence) but saw none of the beautiful fish of Raiatea – of course, there is no reef nor was the water that shallow. Saw white goats on the steep hillsides. Returned for 7 o'clock dinner, joined by P. Moser. Largely fish: magnificent fish soup, *then lobster & tuna, then shrimp & rice, then pink papaya. Moser too found the people distant & will not stay. Also no fresh water in the mountains for him to camp.*

December 23, Monday

Arose at 7:00, disturbed by one of the many ever-cackling roosters. Nowhere to get coffee or any breakfast. Walked the steep hill to Gaughin's grave,[11] set amid a sad assortment of old graves obviously remembered by position, rather than markers. Again noted the dryness of the soil; some leaves of small plants actually curled up. No lush undergrowth as in Tahiti: no large-leafed plants, no <u>large</u> flowers – the plumeria smaller &, of course, the trees fewer. Some quizical or distant faces: I thought Lucien[12] had hard eyes, tho' Greg disagrees. Eyed cautiously as we reached the magazin for biscuits & fruit juice – sparse provisions on the shelves. 2 beer & Arnotts' orange cookies = $3.00 US.

'Atuona: Gaughin's Grave'

In the early afternoon, rested, still hearing children. No rain; strong winds. Rauzy has never inquired if all is well – as Greg said, Victorine's word for him would be "caloulu"[?]. We try to go to Tahuata this afternoon by speed boat.

'Atuona: Bungalows and Chickens'

Same day 6:00

Lucien said (possibly lying) to Greg that gasoline was not available for Tahuata, so we stay another nite.[13] Greg brought Velveeta cheese, bread & juice for lunch & we ate appreciatively. After Greg wrote in his journal, we went for a glorious long walk of 3 miles, west of Atuona. Quietly & completely happy to investigate, take photos, look for a glimpse of distant Tahuata. I was aware to an uncanny degree of Greg: his happiness, his pleasure at realizing, as we walked, that we would arrive at Tahuata at Xmas, like Robarts; his simplicity & innocence kept me startled the whole way, so that the simplicity of a mere walk became total engagement, total absorption in a person – "ambience"[?].

We returned, to buy a tin of meat or beans for tea. Little stock; we found Zwan[14] (spam) more fresh bread, "milk lollipops". When we asked for bananas, a chief was sent off & returned with 13 bananas, at no cost. Meanwhile, the proprietress (one of Rauzy's many establishments, the magazinire [magasiniere?]) told us they'd moved us to the better bungalow. And indeed, our things were in the new, quieter bungalow – even the paperbacks were kept to the same pages, & there were flowers, a sort of double pink sweetpea. We were delighted, pleased at their kindness & our first sign of simple generosity. Now, it is night fall & the sky is luminous white behind the mountain – our 1ˢᵗ day with no rain whatever.

December 25

Banana for breakfast & reading Malraux Days of Hope on Christmas Eve morning. Greg sought out Lucien at 8:00, but was given, again, no assurance of passage to Tahuata. The distance from the villagers remains, & men like Rausy [Rauzy] & Lucien only widen the gulf by their surliness. (Rauzy all excited to sell provisions to 3 young Americans arrived from the Galapagos & anchored in the bay.) In the afternoon, & with another stolid lack of response from Lucien re boats, we went to the convent, looking for Aritana's friends, Sr. Eliz. & Sr. Emanouel [sic]. Came upon Sr. Marietta who spoke English (14 yrs. In New Zealand) & who organized a way for us on Fri. to Tahuata. Her youth & zest seems to give her a good, friendly relationship with families – we do not know how we will return.

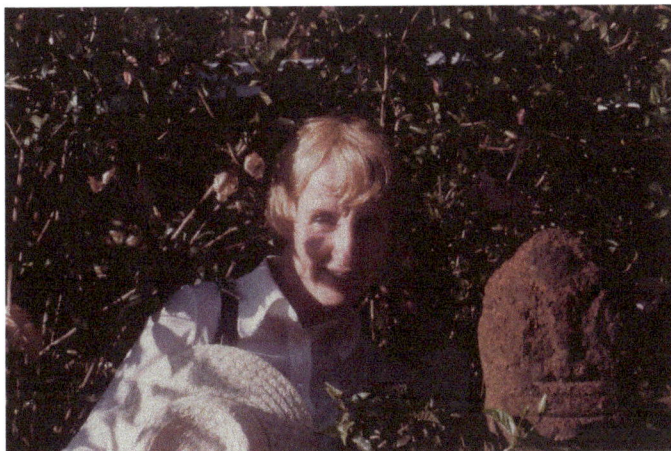

'Atuona: Tiki and Donna'

Had Xmas eve dinner, one of our best: tin of asparagus, bread, rosé, cheese & oranges. Napped until Midnight Mass & just as well one didn't wish to read, for the electricity went off. "Dressed" for Mass in the dark, fumbling for matches. People at Mass – largely girls of the Sisters' school – did not all sing, as in Tahiti – but sat quite disciplined &, I would say, stolid. A few girls giggled at the barking of the countless hounds hanging about.[15] Few men.[16] Only Sr. Marietta spoke to us after Mass; no sense of joy. No lights, so we were disappointed not to open Virginia's[17] gifts. Because of Rauzy's indifference, could have felt like Mary & Joseph in the stable.

Today, we awoke happily, still aware of the paradox of Xmas here. Breakfast of oranges & Arnotts Scotch Fingers; all quiet again; we left quite alone. Walked to the beach & saw a small shark near the shore. No boats; nothing stirring, except the roosters, discovered more paepae & tikis. Animals look hungry & vegetation desperately in need of water. Returned for "Christmas dinner" i.e. tin of Armour meat, cheese, bread, water, sweet biscuit. Not enough activity for me, but we'll save our money for horse back trips for Nukahiva [Nukuhiva] &, in all, we are enormously happy. Opened Virginia's gifts at breakfast: a clever penknife for Greg & a lovely Victorian broach for me. I look forward to "dinner" this evening: mince, pork-&-beans, bread & a tin of fruit salad – w. one spoon.

'Atuona: Paepae (Atikua?) Tohua'

December 26

Yesterday afternoon was delicious: not only for the much-needed exercise but also because our long 3-mile walk into the depths of the valley widened one's whole notion of the village. For the vegetation behind the village is very dense, esp. where villagers have over the many years planted banan[a], coconut, mango, taro, etc. along the river. We followed the road & then a horse-trail along the river, because being acutely aware of the antiquity of the place as we were faced with large stones, traces of lava flows, atua, etc. No insect life to speak of; horses tethered casually along the path. The trail leads with increasing difficulty to the next valley, a trip on horseback, so we were told, of 3 hours. On the return, encountered a Marquesan man of c 30 years, very reminiscent of the tatood man. He kindly showed us an easy trail in one place & talked with us – for his guttural French & hairlip, I dubbed him the Marquesan Frank Strahan.[18] He was born in Tahuata & clearly pleased when Greg mentioned we were off Fri. to see his village. He worked on the road, indicated he collected coconut high on the mountain & pointed toward the mountain ahua. Saw women washing in the river; one fellow drunk; an exhilarating experience.

Christmas dinner was very beautiful, tho' had we not got our few provisions, we'd have gone hungry. Learned to use the kerosene lamp lest Rauzy turn off the electricity early in the night again.

Slept marvelously well & rose early, to sunshine. Cloudy morning, but we walked again on the rocks near the beach, noticing "lizards" tiny black or speckled "fish" of no more than 4 inches which live *as well on land as in the water, preferring jumping from rock to rock, to swimming. Fewer land crabs than Tahiti; no holes along the beaches. Few birds, only an occasional sea birds [sic]. Few fishermen; one <u>very</u> seldom sees a boat of any sort & where they are docked are only 4 or 5. Quietest place – not in terms only of noise, but activity.*

Same day. Hiked into the mountains again, this time on a ridge extending west into the valley & then along a higher ridge, returning toward the village. Only the occasional sound of birds, falling coconut, a child's voice in the valley; no passers-by on the newly cut road or trail. Really exhilarating – the ahu[19] every ½ miles [sic], very large ones, alway[s] the mountain above. Coconut planted ½ way up. Drank from a mountain stream. Greg adoring it all & feeling fit. Tired this time when we returned. Tin of salmon for tea & bread & wine. No fresh fruit. Spent $29.[00] on food for 5 days: outrageous but good going here!

'Vaitahu: From Landing Place'

December 27, Friday

This is a day I scarcely want to describe, or remember. Right now, I am writing sitting on the bed in the home of our Tahuatan friend [Teifitu Gregoire (Gregory) Umu], a very old man slightly crippled by severe elephantiasis.[20] But to think of today. We arose, not having slept well because of excitement at the image of our trip to Tahuata. Finished our chocolate cookies, bread & cheese for breakfast, packed carefully – for example, getting my purse into the fleabag – & left in a slight drizzle for the home of Melanie & Tearo.[21] The gathering of us & them

72

into the jeep to reach the bay nearby was a curious sight; 8 children, their household possessions, us & a pig, trussed: We arrived happily enough – the children named Jacqueline, Sylvie, Norbert, Albert. We loaded all abo[a]rd a sturdy row-boat with an outboard engine. We were pushed out by friends. Then it rained very, very hard & I began to worry for Greg's camera. Clearly – & it became clearer – we had not reckoned on the strenuousness of the journey. In the now driving rain, we made our way into open seas, the children now huddling frightened & nauseated under the front covering. One child took Greg's camera – alone saving it from certain damage. We hit very high waves, 7 foot, dark & turbulent & immensely frightening in the rain & dark clouds. Twenty-five minutes out, truly horrified at the seas, the motor quite suddenly stopped.[22] We drifted while Taero worked uselessly – the motor sounded weaker than the cheapest lawnmower! Melanie showed no fear, so I was calmed a bit; the poor children were sick. Without panic or anger, Taero worked but finally gave up, & he & Greg set slowly (deliberately slowly, for it would be a long row) to rowing. We were, I'd estimate, 1 mile beyond the island in Atuona's bay &, at [as] we *learned later, just before the most cruel & terrifying seas of the trip. On utterly, incredibly good chance, Melanie – a most remarkable woman – stood at the wheel & saw a boat passing in the distance, farther out to sea. As it eventuated, it was the mayor of Vaitahu & M's own father. They towed us (drearily, to me) ashore.[23] And the family determined to set out again, in the afternoon – the children stood around languidly, stolidly eating candies; we were driven back to our bungalow & entered sick & disspirited [sic] &, – me, at least – still trembling inside. As it was now noon, the magazin was closed, we dried our soaked clothes & waited to buy lunch. When we did so at 2:00, Rauzy's wife, hearing our tale, suddenly recalled that the mayor of T. was returning at 3:30. She spoke to Rauzy, & we had a place! (It is said to cost $100.[00]) Again then – this time at 3:00 we set out for Tahuata. We waited 1 hour, met a lovely American yachtsman, seemed to be once again disappointed, as it seemed the mayor had arbitrarily decided to leave us behind. We were finally picked up & carried to the launching "ramp" in a jeep. Then we boarded with Gregoire, a helmsman, the mayor & 2 women, pleased to be on our way.[24]*

'Vaitahu: Village Path'

And the weather <u>was</u> better, the seas had dropped in ferocity, the sun was shining; 4:30. Still it was, to me, terrifying, truly terrifying, at times: twice the engine cut out, once very near the treacherous point on Hiva Oa going across to Tahuata & again in the channel between the two islands. Flying fish & a very beautiful sunset, but again, the motor cut out & we drifted while it was repaired. Still, I was very, very glad that the little boat of Tearo's had quit when it had: it is too terrifying to conceive of rounding the point in his craft. Vaitahu was spectacular, tho' in passing along the dry side of the island we'd seen much very

75

*barren landscape. On landing, we were joyously
greeted by Melanie & her family (they'd just arrived)
her mother.[25] Easily, she helped us arrange lodging
– as it turned out in a house of Gregory's.[26] I'll never
forget him: a strong face & strong, full body – full of
courage & kindness & practical sense. I loved the
appearance of the village more than Atuona: more
open like its people, houses nestled together (unlike
Atuona) as tho' they enjoyed one another, bands of
welcoming children, a jolly walk past houses, petite
churches, up to the house of Gregory.[27] Tho' it was
blissful to be on land, the house was a disturbingly
barren & derelict place, permeated by the odour of
something dead.[28] It looked – or so I evaluated it
late that night – like a Walker Evans picture of the
Gudger house,[29] or a ghetto dwelling, or one of the
stone farmhouses around which the Spanish Civil
War was fought.*

'Vaitahu: Old Paepae Present Dwellings'

What kept in my mind the long & fairly sleepless night, later was how totally one must relinquish one's own values & sensibilities & take on those of the new people: their sense of danger (thus, to Melanie, the crossing to Tahuata was not dangerous), of cleanliness, of privacy (just as Greg & I began to fall asleep, Gregory returned, knocked & while I lay on the bed in only my green nitegown, he rummaged about for rifle bullets & the gun with which his son would go shooting cattle[)].

December 28, Saturday

Rose at 6:00, having been awake for a long time. Heard a child singing Polly-Wolly-Doodle ... a cat jumped thru' the window into the kitchen; used all my perfume to allay the decaying smell; the wind gusts almost with precision regularity [regularly], every 7 minutes; the lizard I felt would remain <u>high</u> on the wall looking for flies &, besides, I am now frightened only of the sea, moreso than planes. No, I am frightened here of contracting elephantiasis or some disease like Thomasita's.[30] These days are waves of deep anxiety: yesterday, convinced that the mayor had neglected us – fears for Greg: rain, little light, the light meter of the camera, water on the camera, too little money, now the return to Hiva Oa, the crossing from Ua Huka to Nukahiva for 4 hours retching constantly. I will be so pleased to return to Atuona, then one week to the Pan Am flight. It is 7:30; a girl brought weak coffee & I'm frightened of the cups. It is raining, but the island's vegetation shows clearly that there are not long hours of rainfall. In fact, there is a rainbow; I pray for good weather tomorrow morning. My period started, making me sad.[31]

'Vaitahu: Children and Research Assistant'[32]

Vaitahu: The Expedition

Saturday, 4:45

Walked far into the valley with Gregoire & felt the fear of disease, dirt leaving me as, a), it was useless & b) Gregoire was so kind & Greg weapt [wept] in his descriptions of historic events.[33] I find myself thinking in French again. The many children – only some of them his grandchildren – crowded into the house, curious to see us, accustomed to roaming thru Gregoire's house. Had our oranges for breakfast, but G. also sent us coffee. On the return of the walk into [the] valley, we were greeted by a woman whose daughter attends school at Atuona. She gave us a bunch of banana[s], tho' her house was as poor (a set of shacks) as any Mexican hovel. (I offered the band of children who surrounded us banana but they prefer mango[)]. G. joined us for lunch, which his daughter-in-law provided: poipoi,[34] beef (very tough) & beans, fish marinated, beer & bread. I trembled at the dirty glasses but was unable to wash them before G poured beer. Took a siesta; Greg said he <u>loves</u> it all. The water runs off & on; we wash in a stone basin outside. Finished Malraux's <u>Days of Hope</u>; walked along the ridge above the sea to the nearby bay. Returned, watching 10-12 men playing bowls. Greg beaming to watch them, & he appears to have *many good pictures. We return to Atuona tomorrow after Mass – it seems to be the only set time for any activity. The sea sounds loudly – when the waves recede, they pull back into to [the] sea hundreds of rocks, sounding like thousands of rifle shots.*

December 29, Sunday

Last evening we enjoyed the most friendly, charming evening, a quite spontaneous evening with the children nearby and Gregoire's daughter-in-law & another woman. It began with dinner: Marie-Ange had brought beef, Gregoire came with a list of the village families, & came the entourage of children, watching us eat but at a slight, courteous distance. After dinner, Greg & Gregoire went to arrange passage to Atuona, at the same time the lights failed. Still the children, &, by now, their mothers had gathered & I found myself explaining Greg's book – especially the maps – to Jean-Jacques, Syprian [Cyprian] & Marie-Ange by the light of the kerosene lamp. They were thrilled & with great concentration studied the pictures of the bays, rivers, mountains.

'Teifitu Uma'

When Greg returned, he instructed the children about the maps; the women & children seemed to wish to stay, one sitting at the doorway smoking some sort of grass but certainly not tobacco – she had many of them. Syprian got his ukulele (he strums it continually) & timidly sang, French songs. Girls, Marie-Lovena, were made to dance for us, half-wanting too but tearful with timidity. I danced a bit; Gregoire's daughter-in-law waltzed with me, enjoying it. They lingered a long while, eating candies kept in our bedroom. One by one the children dropped to sleep on the double bed *in the front room where we were. We could then speak with the women, They, it seemed to me, were slightly restless with the small village or at least recognized some of its restrictions. They seemed to characterize their lives as making poipoi daily & having children, <u>large</u> families. They were certain we were rich – none had seen the Sunday service at Atuona. They were interested in Papeete, where many young men of the islands go to work – & prices of food. Suddenly, they left; it was all quite wonderful. During the night, the wind came up – a lizard above our heads making gurgling[35]*

TEUPOO TOEE = lady with cigarette[36]

Children of Vaitahu in the pictures

Marie-Claire in blue

Marie-LOVENA in green

Jean-Jacques in green shirt

Terri – in red shirt

Syprian in striped shirt

Marie-Ange in yellow dress

Lucie – in darker green

Marguerite – pale blue

Marie-Yvonne – infant

Tatiana – brown

Mary-Florence – blue blouse (tall)

Marie-Angele – small & in pink

---

sounds.

This morning we attended prayers at the church, after taking many pictures of the children, all of Gregoire's family, Syprian, & the children of Teupoo Toee. They were beautifully dressed for church, & so very excited to be photographed that they arrived at 6:45!

The prayers were, again, a unique experience. I was convinced that the first series of prayers – chanted at an increasing tempo in a very low register & done in Marquesan – created quite an erotic effect, a most sensuous exhilarating sensation I felt thru'out. The rhythms seemed to increase in intensity, recede, & again become intense. Could imagine well the totally drugging effect of earlier Marquesan chanting. The remaining music was

Sankey-ish or sentimental French hymnology, like St. Joseph parish in Faaa. Children occupied the front benches, sexes separated; similarly separated the adults behind. A shark-eyed old man, the sexton, kept the children under surveillance. Some men's shirts had the folds of new apparel: clearly Xmas gifts. Offerings were made during the final hymns, the small boys first, then girls, then women w. babes, then men. The coins were placed in a tray held by a plastic angel at the creche: the head bobbed– presumably in thanks – as money was dropped.

TEARO NEUFFER[37]

We left the church happy & eager to take the boat to Atuona. But the mayor had other plans for the boat &, against his word, disappointed us. We leave with Taero at 3, all going well.

December 30, Monday.

Yesterday was perhaps our most difficult day. Feeling betrayed by the mayor & uncertain of transport to Atuona, we returned to Gregoire's house, despondent to re-enter that house, promised passage with Tearo at 3 o'clock. The children followed us, as did TEIEFITU [Teifitu] who was disappointed for us. Marie-Ange brought lunch, setting it out in the horrible kitchen: boiled banana, more beef, tea – & she set out also – as a matter of course – the now-rancid beef & poipoi of yesterday. I could not eat for the smell & dirt & distress. Somehow the long hours to 2:00 passed; the children, after pouring [poring] excitedly over the pictures in Lash's Eleanor[38], left for swimming (that & cards & marbles & reading the same books continually seems their only recreation[)]. Teiefitu met us & walked to the sea with [us]: the mayor not in sight. The time at the sea went quickly: the children posed in the water for a photo & again on the boat. I gave Marie-Ange & Marie-Florence my bracelets. Taero came promptly & confidently; we bid farewell to dear Teiefitu & the children.[39] On the return to Atuona at 3:00 the sea was calm. Taero demonstrated his prowess with the boat steering thru' close rock formations. We stopped at a very small valley where he deposited banana & mango, preparing for days camping there with Melanie & the children. Just at the point & some 15 feet from the black rocks, the engine cut out. I felt hopeless fear again, but we did not move into the rocks, & the motor responded. Taero dropped us at the ramp &, very wet & caked with sea-spray, we returned to our bungalow hoping Rauzy had not disposs[ess]ed us. As the magazin was closed, we had dinner at Rauzy's restaurant but again the main course was shrimp, so Greg ate little.[40] The usual kittens crept from table to table – as at the Chinese restaurant at Taravao & here in Nukahiva. We slept well.

On Monday, December 30, we arose early, excited to leave for Nukahiva – it was to take us from 7:30 to 3:15 to make the entire journey! The "elite" of the French-born society of Atuona gathered round the pilots & bade farewell. In the jeep, we returned to the airport, encountering some rain. I felt a bit the outsider, as most of the time at Atuona. Still Rauzy had charged us very reasonably (7200 Polynesian) & even informed us there was breakfast – our first coffee (with milk!) since Aritana's. Stale bread but delicious. The flight was good: few passengers & Greg got some good photos. The pilot was kind,

pointing out to Greg the island of Ua Huka ahead –
so he could peer through their windscreens.

'Ua Huka: Airport'

Ua H. was barren & I was happy it was not to be our
resting place for a week.[41] In the "airport" a woman
from New Caledonia gave us leis & biscuits, & we
met Brother Premont. Greg is able now to speak
French with some fluency. Suddenly – to take the
departing plane – came Moser, a comical delightful
fellow who'd stayed at Ua Huka & discovered tikis
& a funeral piroque.[42] Meanwhile a jeep arrived for

us & we began what proved to be a very dangerous descent from the landing strip to the bay; the roads were slippery w. rainwater yet followed the very ridges of the mountain. The arrival at & departure in the landing-craft type boat was exhilarating, another high spot & exciting experience. We waded to the small boat & were launched to the larger one, finding our way up to the cabin above.[43] Perfectly gorgeous deep bay with spectacular caves, & the seas blue-green & calm. We passed a rookery for seabirds.[44] About 45 minutes out from Nukahiva, 10 or so dolphins began to play in the wash of the ship – stayed with us for 20 or 30 minutes.[45] Tipevai [Taipivai] Bay was beautiful[46] but Taiohe [Taiohae] is spectacular, a scene of immense grandeur.[47]

'Nukuhiva: Sth Coast'

The boat anchored at a wharf & we need not pay, as it is included in the air fare. (M. Rauzy now seemed less onerous to me, as we realized he too was a UTA employee, responsible for all "on the ground" at Atuona.) On landing the most unforgettably marvelous & surprising event occurred. Our fellow-passenger, the brother, had been met by the Picpus Fathers & the bishop.[48] After introductions, the bishop turned to Greg, introduced himself & when Greg offered his name, the bishop dissolved into excitement, recognizing the editor of R[obart]'s journal![49] So grand! Treated, then, as dignitaries, he insisted on finding a house for us (& fortunately for there are few, if any, tourist accom.)⁵⁰ & did so at the house of Philomena – a jolly, clean & beautifully situated house, build [built] on the paepae of Kaatonui [Kiatonui].⁵¹ We later went for a promenade, meeting some American yachtsmen & one from Toorak!

'Taiohae: Philomene's'

The bay is so lovely: high mountain & cliffs, white sandy beaches, breath-taking flame-trees.[52] 30 dwellings in sight: on the right, the French Administrative center, on the left (Avenue de Durdilon [Dordillon]) the church, school & bishop's home.[53] Finally we set out for tea, & found it, the single restaurant, offering meals only at 8. Walked to the fort;[54] returned to restaurant where 2 tables of the many were set: Tahitian music, (tinned) mushroom soup, gorgeous fried fish w. limes & onion, fresh bread & lots of water, melon. All for $4.00!! Great expectations at this magnificent place.

December 31.

Very hot day. Had our oranges (from Rauzy's supper) for lunch – first & wrote in our journals. Did our wash & have it out in sunshine. Feel the memory of Vaitahu fading. Walked to the fort for pictures, then along the beach beyond: bright blue fish. Returned & bought lunch at Chinese magazin: cheese, crackers, sprite, sweet biscuits, aspro (we have sore throats) & candy. Looks like Myers[55] compared to Atuona or – Vaitahu![56]

'Taiohae: NE Sector'

Sunday, January 4[57]

Today we leave Nukuhiva, at 8 when the boat departs for Uoo-a-puh [Ua Pou] & then to Ua Huka. We are very ready to go because we have been completely immobile here. On Thurs. & Fri. morning, Greg worked in the archives;[58] I managed to find some lettuce & a cucumber & vinegar for lunch, & G. was overjoyed.

'Taiohae: Cathedral'

Otherwise we have had grapefruit (last 2 days) &
sweet biscuits for breakfast & only cheese, crackers
& sometimes grapefruit for lunch – & Tang! Adille &
Alain Le Cleash [Cléac'h] have been most kind to us;
we had an aparatif [aperitif] with them Thurs. night
& then found the restaurant open: the meals were:
1) soup & fish 2) watery soup (but salt & pepper)
& 3 fried eggs & cake; 3) same soup & some kind
of awful beef & noodles. We retire immediately after
tea because Philomena turns off the electricity early
& the kerosene lamp is insufficient. We give over the

*back part of the house to the rats, & use the grass
instead of the toilet. Lovely dinner at Adille's Sat:
fondu with beef filet & vegetables. Beaut cake & –
ice cream! And coffee! Greg is good but eager also
to leave.*

Sunday, Jan 3rd (?)[59]

*Rose early, a windy night. Had breakfast of Tang &
(for me) the avocado given by Adille & grapefruit
for Greg. Arrived for mass slightly early – the
congregation awaits the bells before entering. A new
cathedral underway – the bishop says he needs a good
architect. Mass most moving, to me. Tho' distracted
by the lovliest Polynesian infant, I was attentive to
monsignor's sermon, on the Epiphany. Noted the
authentic Marquesan design wherever possible: the
symbol of the lizard, the magnificent statue of the
Virgin. Met Stanislaus after Mass – no trip to Tipevai
& I was disappointed for Greg. Had Sunday dinner
with the bishop, Adille, Alain, 3 brothers, Laurent
Prémont & Jean. Beaut meal & quiet, interesting
conversation.[60] Saw Msgr's artefacts once again & he
explained the difficulties of mission life, Marquesan*

language, etc. Greg not too well; going for a late afternoon swim, we met John, the young yachtsman we'd met fleetingly at Atuona. On his return from town, he took us to "Mahana" to exchange for a copy of Greg's book a tiki from Hapatoni.[61] Shoving out for the yacht I was soaked, forcing me to wear the green skirt instead of slacks on the boat, as I'd intended. Seasick immediately on John's yacht & fearful for the 8 o'clock departure.

'Taiohae: Greg as Anthrop[ologist] on Pikivehine'

Jan 6 [i.e. 7], Tuesday, aboard Pan Am, 10:35.

Arrived at the airport after a lovely dinner at Maeva: taro, feu, sweet potato – chocolate mousse! Enjoyed the day at Maeva: the carpeting, clean towels, fragrant soap, clean sheets, privacy. The boat trip from Nukuhiva had been a nightmare for both of us. The bishop collected Greg, Laurent & me, & together with Adille, Jean, Alain, etc. presented us with leis of shells – they'd had prayers at 6 & prayed for Greg as he was working for the Marquesan people. Happy as we watched the lights of Nukuhiva disappear, tho' just boarding the Kahoa [Kaoha] Nui was like mounting into a giant tub. Hit the open sea, some rain & strong high waves on the side ... the boat pitching, rolling & lunging.[62] Impossible to walk safely on the deck – a poor family in the head, all children & mother already terrified & sick. Felt like I was unimaginably on some 19th c. Chinese junk. All passengers looked dazed, then all terribly sick. By 8:45, Greg & me very sick; I clung to a pale rear canvas covering at the side – Greg in front, so sick. Got sicker, went downstairs, got weaker & clung to a metal catch at the very back of the boat, worried that Greg would miss me.[63] Greg joined me; both sick to Uapou [Ua

Pou].[64] There Greg spotted a flat leather mat on the floor in what turned out to be the ship's kitchen. He led me there in the dark & I curled up by the wet steel wall but it was comforting & the mat soft. Got Greg to join me: I kept on all the shells considering them the good will & blessings of our friends at Nukuhiva & always will. Kept repeating to myself "The Lord is my shepherd" & believing it – together with the feel of Greg alongside, the hours from Uapou to Ua Huka were filled with more contentment than just the peace of not being sick.[65] Felt like I was on the tongue of a large large whale, gamboling forward – rhythmic lunges. Aware of slowly pulling into the bay at Ua Huka at 5:45. Most passengers had got off at Uapou however very sick too. Hard, to adjust to the calm; still shaking & weak & always the worry of getting out of Ua Huka. Had breakfast in the captain's kitchen: the most marvellous hot tea & hot slices of bread & butter.[66] The administrator, André the mayor of Uapou, we 3, the captain. Awaited the small boat to get ashore – all took our shoes & sox off again; awaited the jeep; waited at Moser's "pension" with more good coffee in filthy cups. Learned there were 11 passengers for 8 places & full of fear again. Poor Greg – so many worries.[67] Happily, got a place; last *moments in the Marquesas were a compliment for me from the ship's captain, a woman with leis & <u>cold</u> (!) coconut juice. Good flight; nice lunch; flying LOW after Manihi but no troubles, eager for a shower at Maeva. Taxi to hotel & beautiful room,[68] soon filled with smell of fish from our suitcase[69] & Greg's shell. Lovely dinner; very tired – stiff neck & bruise from the side of the ship, felt rolling motion of the ship most of the night. Today bought book & lithographs, visited w. Aritana, & finally got away from 633.[70] Greg bought me French perfume; has a headache. So good to me.*

POSTFACE

The journal you have just read was written as a private record of Greg's and my time together in the Society Islands and Marquesas at the end of 1974 and the start of 1975. Nearly half a century later, I am pleased that it is now to be published. It takes us back to a time which was then the present, rather than the past. As Ron Adams has noted in his Preface – quoting Greg – diaries (or journals) catch, in a way that written-up histories cannot, the bleak days, the chance discoveries, the opportunistic sallies, the fumbling questions, and the occasional days of light and excitement. All of those contingencies are part of the reality with which historians contend and as such they deserve to be on the public record.

My thanks go to Ron Adams for editing the manuscript. Like Greg before him, Ron admires the peoples of the Pacific and loves writing about them. I am deeply grateful. I am also grateful and moved by Joy Damousi's generous Foreword. The three of us – Joy, Ron and I – are close friends as well as colleagues, and their active involvement in this project has given me much joy.

Donna Merwick Dening

13th February 2020

NOTES

1 Presumably a descendant of magistrate and lawyer Alexandre Holozet 1823-1895. O'Reilly *Tahitiens*: 263-4.

2 Suburb of Papeete.

3 Nguyen Van-Cam 1875-1929, a political deportee, arrived in Tahiti in 1898 and was exiled by order of Governor-General Doumer to the Marquesas. An infirmier volant and government agent, he returned to Papeete in 1911 to establish the military hospital pharmacy, a post he held until his death. A friend of Gaughin, together they wrote a comedy in three acts: *Les Amours d'un Vieux Peintre aux Îles Marquises*. He married Punu Ura a Tamitiau from Bora Bora and had two children, including Pierre Napoléon (Peter), who married Jeanne Lequerré, with whom he had three children. O'Reilly *Tahitiens*: 580-1.

4 Rest of page and following page blank. The reference to Raiatea indicates that the Reflection was written after December 19.

5 Rest of page blank.

6 Donna and Greg's only child, born 20 December 1973 and died 24 December 1973.

7 "I am flying over an immense ocean. ... Actually I am sitting nervously behind two gesticulating French pilots. They point to every button on their instrument panel as if it is a subject of some great philosophical or mechanical crisis. It is December 1974. We have just taken off from Tahiti's Faa airport in a wet season storm. We are over this vast ocean on a northeast tack. That small part of it beneath

our northeast flight over the 950 miles separating Tahiti from the Marquesas was the northern tip of the Tuamotu ... Archipelago. ..." *Beach Crossings*: 57

8 "I had failed rather badly in the photography classes I had taken in preparation for my visit to the Fenua'enata. I had been too timid to enter the private space of those 'interesting' faces of the poor and old and eccentric my teachers wanted me to invade. Now as the pilots begin to tap their compass and reach for their binoculars, I find my timidity is returning.

Still I have my camera in my hand as we approached The Land, and my face pressed against the cabin porthole. Suddenly, through a gap in the clouds, I realise I am looking down on the one place in all The Land I had wanted to see, Vaitahu Bay on the island of Tahuatu. ... I have a slide of my first sighting of a beach that has meant so much to me. It is a precious slide. Fading, though." *Beach Crossings*: 58-9

9 "The landing-strip [on Hiva Oa] looks as long and wide as an aircraft carrier. It is on the top of a ridge behind the village and beach of Atuona." *Beach Crossings*: 59

10 Guy Rauzy, born 1933, teacher and trader, member of the Territorial Assembly 1957, 1967 and 1972, and Mayor of Atuona 1972. Noted for his efforts in pushing for the commissioning of aerodromes in the Marquesas to compensate for the decline of maritime transport. O'Reilly, *Tahitiens:* 481

11 "We paid Gaughin honour. We walked up the hill of Hueakihi to the cemetery. His grave is easily seen. Amid white cement tombs open to the sun, his is of reddish rocks and shaded by a frangipani tree. Seventy-five years after his death one of Gaughin's final wishes was granted. The cast of a favourite work, a ceramic sculpture he had called *Oviri,* was placed on his grave." *Beach Crossings*: 62

12 A local store-owner. See *Islands and Beaches*: 1

13 "Those last miles to Vaitahu were to prove harder to make

than we had thought. It was a few days before Christmas. The islands had succumbed to a deeper level of quiet. There was a gasoline shortage, too. No one could guarantee a return from Tahuata to Atuona." *Beach Crossings*: 61

14 Brand of luncheon meat.

15 This sentence is inserted at top of page.

16 "When we went to midnight mass on Christmas Eve, Vatican Council II was eerily present in a distant way. The mass was demystified. The secret language of Latin was gone. The altar of sacrifice had become a table for communion. The priest's gestures and demeanour were open and inclusive, not divisive and self-important. But there was division nonetheless. The de'Latinised liturgy was doubly vernacular—French and Marquesan. Every French prayer and reading had a Marquesan echo. On the left of the church sat the sisters and the girls of the boarding school. On the right sat the Atuona community. The left was all French, hymns as well. The right was all Marquesan, hymns as well." *Beach Crossings*: 63.

17 Virginia and Douglas Kennedy were close friends in Melbourne and part of the same Catholic discussion group.

18 University of Melbourne archivist, 1930-2003.

19 Polynesian stone structures, often associated with marae.

20 "I met the old man Teifitu the day after Christmas 1974. Meeting him made me decide to write this book the way it is. We had first seen him, my wife and I, as we waited like him on the steps of Lucien's trade-store at Atuona on Hiva Oa. He sat on the doorsteps, knees high, his sandals uncovering swollen feet, his eyes rheumy behind the thick lenses of his glasses, his smiles distant in the way old men's smiles sometimes are, as if he did not quite hear. He joked with the young men who drank beer in the shade until one by one they went off into the heat on a horse or with a dog in a jeep that raised the dust on the road, and he was alone with

a parcel of stick loaves and a box of *vin ordinaire.* " *Islands and Beaches*: 1

21 Greg's 'Taro'. "The sisters on our inquiring [at midnight mass, when inquiring how they might get to Tahuata] said that, yes, there were teachers at the school returning to Tahuata for the Christmas holidays and gave us their names, Melanie and Taro, and where we would find them. Melanie and Taro when we visited them agreed to take us to Tahuata but could not bring us back. In our desperation, we thought we would take the risk of finding another way back." *Beach Crossings*: 63-4

22 "We were travelling to Tuhuata in [Taro and Melanie's] open dinghy when the outboard motor had stopped within a few hundred feet off the black cliffs that are the western end of 'Traitors' Bay'." *Islands and Beaches*: 1

23 "It took us several days to reach Vaitahu, however, and then only after dramatic recues from a drifting, powerless boat we had boarded at Atuona." *Beach Crossings*: 64

"The 'mayor's' boat had rescued us, sick and frightened, and later taken us, with the old man [Teifitu], to Tahuata." *Islands and Beaches*: 1

24 "The old man Teifitu had been 'mayor' of Vaitahu on Tahuata in his time, had been chief, *haka 'iki*, in less civic terms. We learned that quickly in the jokes directed at him and in the half-clowning of his answers. They were different men, the old man and the new 'mayor'. The old man was not made for fibreglass boats, for commerce or for the vigour of new authority. Politicking had passed him by, and there was no market for the sort of knowledge he possessed. In a land dispossessed of all its ways to support itself, the 'mayors' were political beggars to the French. Their past was worthless to their present poverty, but their future was worth a little for the freedom it gave the French to keep an empire and make a nuclear testing-ground." *Islands and Beaches*: 1

25 "We crossed the beach at Vaitahu in total disarray. Our experiences on the water had unsettled us. We needed an aggression for negotiating accommodation and transport that we did not have. Our softness bred distrust." *Beach Crossings*: 64

26 "It was Teifitu who offered us somewhere to stay. We followed him along the rocky path up the valley to his house, which looked back over the palms and breadfruit trees to the sea." *Islands and Beaches*: 1-2

"[A]n old man, Teifitu Umu, took us in hand. He had rheumy eyes and feet swollen with elephantiasis. ... With a shuffling walk he took us up the path beside the stream that flowed down the valley. ... Teifitu was a widower." *Beach Crossings*: 64

27 "The women came and talked with us and teased their convent-educated daughters to dance more freely. They wondered how rich we might be that we could come so far." *Islands and Beaches*: 2

28 "Our appreciation of [Teifitu's] kindness did not displace our dismay at the conditions of his house. But he had given us hospitality and we swallowed our qualms and used it." *Beach Crossings*: 64

29 Pseudonym for 'Burroughs', a tenant farm family photographed by American photographer and photojournalist Walker Evans (1903-1975) for the book he produced with writer James Agee, *Let Us Now Praise Famous Men: Three Tenant Families*, first published in 1941, though Donna probably saw the photograph in the 1969 Panther edition.

30 Thomasita and Donna both belonged to the Order of the Sisters of Charity of the Blessed Virgin Mary and attended University of Wisconsin together. Thomasita suffered from Pemphigus, which causes blisters and sores in the mouth and throat.

31 Because it meant that she was not pregnant.

32 A playful and ironic reference to Donna – just as in other photographs Greg refers to himself as 'Greg as anthropologist'.

33 "Teifitu walked us round the sights and sites of the valley. Behind the beach of rolling stones in a cleared area, a breadfruit tree stands. Somewhere nearby the Spaniards said mass and killed those among Enata who jostled during it. Somewhere nearby they set up three stakes for three bodies. … Deep in the valley at the end of a line of trees is a monument to three French soldiers killed in ambuscade by Enata in 1843. Teifitu showed us where and how the deaths occurred. When I asked him where the monument was for Enata dead, he shrugged his shoulders. No, there were no monuments, but there is memory and there will be history." *Beach Crossings*: 66

"We wandered about the valley and listened to its sombre silence. Teifitu talked with me, wrote out the names of those families still on Tahuata, shared genealogies, was excited to see names he knew in a book he could not read." *Islands and Beaches*: 2

34 In Tahiti and the Marquesas: a paste of cooked or fermented breadfruit or banana with coconut milk, similar to the Hawaiian poi.

35 Space left for names to be added later.

36 Written at the top of the page.

37 Written at top of page.

38 Joseph P. Lash's Pulitzer Prize-winning *Eleanor and Franklin* (1971).

39 "When we left, [Teifitu] was the last we saw." *Islands and Beaches*: 2

40 Because eating shrimp made him ill.

41 "We flew to Ua Huka to join an old French naval landing craft for the five-hour voyage to Nukuhiva. The bare dry

hills of Ua Huka are most untropical, more like Mexico ..."
Beach Crossings: 74

42 "We met up with a Swiss professor who was in high excitement at his time among the 'primitives', his word. '*Crains, crains* [skulls, skulls]', he kept saying—in a canoe in a cave!'" *Beach Crossings*: 74

43 "Our berths on the landing craft, as it were, were a set of paladin-like seats high on the stern. We shared them with a French-Canadian missionary brother coming to inspect the mission schools. The landing craft dragged itself off the beach on its stern anchor and turned out of the cove and along the shore of Ua Huka." *Beach Crossings*: 74

44 "We stopped to pick up some crew members from an islet alive with seabirds. New Year's Eve was on hand and there would be a *koina*, a feast. The crew members had collected a boatload of eggs for it, as their forebears had done for centuries." *Beach Crossings*: 74-6

45 "Then we turned to a hazy blue line of Nikuhiva to the west. It was three hours before we could discern anything of the island's landscape. We approached Nukuhiva from its southeast corner, and could see its north and south coast stretching away. All was abrupt cliff in the blue haze of the sea." *Beach Crossings*: 76

46 "As we moved along the south coast, I began to recognise bays. Taipivai came first. Its valley and the high cliffs that hedge its waters stretch miles back into the hinterland of Nukuhiva." *Beach Crossings*: 76

47 "For me, it was a moment of tense expectancy as we first caught sight of the vertical lines of light-coloured rocks that were the navigators' signpost to the entry of Taiohae Bay. We turned carefully through the narrow entrance and were overwhelmed, as every visitor must be, by the massiveness of the bay's encircling mountain ridge." *Beach Crossings*: 76

48 Mgr Hervé-Marie Le Cléac'h, born 11 March 1915 at Dinéault (Finistère), joined the order of Sacred Hearts in 1933. He was a prisoner in June 1940 and ordained at Chartres December 1943. After teaching in France and Canada, appointed Provincial of the Order in 1958. Appointed administrateur apostolique de Taiohae 8 December 1970 and Bishop of Taiohae 1 March 197. Arrived at Taiohae 7 March 1973. O'Reilly *Tahitiens:* 325-6.

49 "Our companion, the mission brother, was ceremonially welcomed and almost disappeared among the green and purple leis piled high around his neck. We stood off awkwardly, hoping to ask somebody for somewhere to stay. The brother brought us to the bishop [of the Marquesas], Mgr Hervé-Marie Le Cléac'h. Recognition is not something I have come to expect, not then, not now. So let me record, not for the boast of it, but for the pleasure of it, that the bishop when he heard my name said: 'Not *the* Greg Dening'. *The Marquesan Journal of Edward Robarts* had come before me. It was one of the nicest moments of my scholarly and writing life. The bishop embraced me and excitedly went around the crowd telling them who I was and how marvellous *The Marquesan Journal of Edward Robarts*." *Beach Crossings*: 77

"I had a happy welcome at Taiohae by the bishop of the Marquesas, Mgr Hervé-Marie Le Cléac'h. The bishop was a professor of theology before he came to the Land eight years ago. He came with some insight into the changes Vatican Council II had made to the Catholic Church; he came with some determination to let the Men [Marquesans], now Christian, find expression for their faith in the ways of the land." *Islands and Beaches*: 290

50 "The bishop interceded for us with the administrator, a thick-set man in a perfectly creased khaki uniform, about finding us accommodation in the official visitors' residence. But the administrator rebuffed him. We gathered that had we been simple tourists we would have got it, but as I was

a *monsieur*, a person of importance, our non-notification of our coming was taken as a slight. The bishop said that the administrator had been twenty years in Africa, and let us know with a gesture that this was the last outpost of French colonialism." *Beach Crossings*: 77

51 "At the water's edge before us were the ruins of a stone house platform, a *paepae*. I knew immediately that it was that of Putahaii, a powerful woman of Robarts' and Crook's days. She was the mother of the *haka'iki*, the chief, of Taiohae, Kiatonui. ... I sat on the porch of our house that evening, the bay before me, framed by breadfruit trees and Putahaii's *paepae*. ... Our house on the edge of the bay stood on the now dismantled *tohua* of the Hoata valley. Hopu-Au it was called. Down the road from us on Dordillon Avenue, in front of the old cathedral tilting into the ground and the new cathedral beside it, stood a plaza that had been Mauia, the *tohua* of Meau valley. A so-called 'sacrificial altar-stone' on the old *tohua* now sprouts a large crucifix." *Beach Crossings*: 78, 80

52 "Taiohae, with its giant beauty, still enfolds the tiny things that men make. The town at Taiohae still hides behind the trees, or, if one sees it in the summer months, is garlanded with the scarlet brilliance of the flame-trees." *Islands and Beaches*: 289

53 "By the time of our visit the population of Taiohae was some hundreds [instead of the six to nine thousand of 1792 or the mere twenty or thirty of the 1920s], enhanced by the fact that the Catholic mission had established a boys' boarding school there for all the islands of Fenua'enata." *Beach Crossings*: 78

"The road which skirts the shore is divided at a middle point: the half which stretches westward past the bishop's house and mission school is called *Avenue* de Mgr Dordillon; the half which stretches eastward to the gaol, hospital, the offices of the administration and the *residénce* is called *Avenue* d'Admiral Dupetit-Thouars. In the middle ground between west and east, left and right, are two or three *magasins*, a place for entertainment and celebration, a basketball court and a little souvenir market, empty unless a ship comes in." *Islands and Beaches*: 289

54 Fort Collet.

55 A well-known department store in Melbourne.

56 "So we walk the valleys of Taiohae on hot, dusty tracks in January 1975 ... We move around to the western tip ... up to Koueva hidden in the mimosa tangle; over to the hillock where the blockhouse used to stand and Pakoko was executed. We climb back up the cliffs of Pakiu where the ironwood tree of Vahitapu used to stand. Where the French set up their camp, other ruins overlay the old defences now—the remains of prison cells built for the revolutionaries of the Paris Commune, and the foundations for a cathedral that never rose above the ground. Down to Tuhiva, Fort Collet. There we stand, the past of this place all grey-shrouded around us." *Beach Crossings*: 88

57 January 4 was a Saturday.

58 "[In] the house of the bishop ... A museum, an archive, a small library and conversation with a gentle, kindly man attracted me there. ... There are papers of some forty missionaries of the Congregation of the Sacred Hearts of Jesus and Mary in the bishop's archives. ... I have to confess that I retreated to the mission archives in some relief. Archives are my life. I love their cool quiet. Meeting the dead in archives is less traumatic than meeting the living on the beach. These archives looked out on a garden. *Tiki* peered in at me through the greenery ... When the light was right or when I grew stiff at the table, I practised my photography on the *tiki*. ... My notes grow thick. The priests whose diaries and letters I am reading came early in the mission—in 1838—before they could call on the French administration for help." *Beach Crossings*: 88-9

"I worked in the archives of the mission and in its museum and spoke with [Bishop Le Cléac'h] on the porch of his house looking out across the bay beyond its heads to Ua Pou." *Islands and Beaches*: 290

59 The question mark is Donna's. It should be Sunday January 5.

60 "There was some irony in the fact that our last meal in The Land was our largest and most delicious. The staff of the mission school and the bishop entertained us with gracious hospitality. It was ironic because we were about to lose every bit of it a few hours later as we returned to Ua Huka to catch the plane back to Tahiti." *Beach Crossings*: 90

61 A small coastal village to the south of Vaitahu notable for the ancient ruins of the two large meeting and worshipping sites of Me'ae Anapara and Me'ae Eiaa.

62 "We had to make for Ua Puo to pick up more passengers before trying for Ua Huka. The first part of our dog-leg voyage was across the seas and the weather. Instantly *Kaoha Nui* began to corkscrew in an alarming fashion. The stars were gone in a few minutes, hidden by the spray from the bow and rain on the wind. ... Dinner was gone in two minutes, and a hundred times over in the next three hours." *Beach Crossings*: 90-1

63 "Seasickness is the most selfish of all complaints. There was no room in my self-pity for anybody else. I clung to a stanchion and leant over the railing every few minutes—on the lee-side, of course. ... I was hardly conscious, till I looked up and saw that Donna, my partner, who had been clinging to another stanchion was gone. So was everybody else. In terror that something had happened to her, I crawled over the unwalkable deck. I tumbled down the stairs and went around the passengers who looked like they were on some Stygian crossing. No one had seen her. I went to what passed as a toilet on the *Kaoha Nui*. At that moment Donna came out the door." *Beach Crossings*: 91

64 "I cannot really describe how she looked. She had just plucked up the courage to put her hand through all the filth in the washbowl to pull out the plug and had discovered why the plug was there. There was no pipe connected to the bowl. The filth had flowed all over her. We crawled around till we found space enough for our two bodies on the floor of the cabin." *Beach Crossings*: 91

65 "After that … the *Kaoha Nui* turned into the weather toward Ua Huka. It will be hard ever to forget the euphoria we felt in the windless calm of dawn and the still of the bay at Ua Huka." *Beach Crossings*: 91

66 "Someone gave us a cup of coffee and a croissant." *Beach Crossings*: 91

67 "There had been one more moment of crisis at the 'airport' at Ua Huka when we discovered that out plane had been overbooked. For a time we feared that all our troubles to get to The Land would be repeated in trying to get away from it. Somehow we got on the plane." *Beach Crossings*: 91-2

68 "We thought we were deserving of some 'rest and recreation' after our expedition. So we booked ourselves into a Tahitian resort hotel which we could barely afford. The look on the hotel porter's face when he took our smelly bags and looked at our clothing still unchanged from our night on the *Kaoha Nui* told us we were crossing another sort of beach." *Beach Crossings*: 92

69 "[O]n the plane … they put our jiffy-bag luggage in the hold under a parcel of fresh fish." *Beach Crossings*: 92

70 Possibly refers to the flight number.

APPENDIX

LIST OF GREG DENING PHOTOGRAPHS
DECEMBER 1974-JANUARY 1975

To prepare for his trip to the Marquesas at the end of 1974, Greg purchased a camera and enrolled in photography classes – which, he later noted (*Beach Crossings:* 58), he 'failed rather badly'. That did not, however, deter him from taking hundreds of photographs in the Society and Marquesas Islands. Nearly all were taken by Greg, though a few – when he was the subject – were shot by Donna. Very occasionally a third person took a photograph of Greg and Donna together. Together with Donna's original Journal, the photographs have been deposited in the Pacific Collection at the University of Hawai'i-Manoa Library, where they are available for reference. In the following list they are grouped according to Greg and Donna's itinerary: Tahiti, Moorea, Huahine, Raiatea and Tahaa in the Society Islands, Manihi in the Tuamotu Archipelago for a refuelling stop, and Hiva Oa, Tahuata, Ua Huka and Nukuhiva in the Marquesas Islands.

The captions are as Greg wrote them on the 35mm slide mounts. Some slides bear the same caption: these are not duplicates but different photographs of the same subject, often taken in quick succession with almost imperceptible differences. Under each island heading, the captions are arranged alphabetically.

TAHITI
[Untitled beach scene]
[Untitled: Over water at night towards monument]
[Untitled: Over water at night towards shore]
Aritana
Aritiana Vict Anthrop
Matavai Bay: From Air
Matavai Bay: From Air
Tahiti: Airstrip
Tahiti: Arahurahu
Tahiti: Arahurahu: Tiki
Tahiti: Aritana & Mangos
Tahiti: Aritana Holozet
Tahiti: Arue: Prop. of Pomare
Tahiti: Arue: Pt Honu
Tahiti: Basin Plastique
Tahiti: Faa
Tahiti: Faa & Taapuna
Tahiti: Fare Arahurahu Fata Tupapo
Tahiti: Fare Arahurahu Fata Tupapo
Tahiti: Mahaiatea
Tahiti: Mahaiatea
Tahiti: Mahaiatea
Tahiti: Manoo: Fa
Tahiti: Marae Arahurahu
Tahiti: Marae Arahurahu Tiki
Tahiti: Matavai Back Mts
Tahiti: Matavai Bay Beach
Tahiti: Matavai Bay from Tahara'a
Tahiti: Matavai Beach & Mts
Tahiti: Matavai Beach & Mts
Tahiti: Matavai from Tahara'a
Tahiti: Matavai Lighthouse
Tahiti: Matavai Looking W
Tahiti: Matavai W. Slopes

Tahiti: Nth Coast from Arahoho
Tahiti: Pt Arahoho
Tahiti: Raiuauae Statue
Tahiti: Raiuauae Statue
Tahiti: SE Coast
Tahiti: SE Coast
Tahiti: Sunset
Tahiti: Tahara'a & Pupotea
Tahiti: Taiarapu
Tahiti: Tautira
Tahiti: Tautira Spanish Mission
Tahiti: Toanui
Tahiti: Tomb of Pomare V
Tahiti: Tomb of Pomare V
Tahiti: Tomb of Pomare V
Tahiti: Tomb of Pomare V
Tahiti: Vaitepihi
Tahiti: W. from Tahara'a

MOOREA
[Untitled: from air]
[Untitled: island and reef from air]
[Untitled: island and reef from air]
[Untitled: island and reef from air]
[Untitled: landscape]
Moorea
Moorea
Moorea
Moorea
Moorea
Moorea Sunset
Moorea: Afareaitu from Air
Moorea: Air
Moorea: Air

Moorea: Air
Moorea: Air
Moorea: Air
Moorea: Air
Moorea: Airport from Air
Moorea: Cook's Bay
Moorea: Cook's Bay
Moorea: Cook's Bay
Moorea: Cook's Bay
Moorea: Cook's Bay
Moorea: Cook's Bay
Moorea: Cook's Bay
Moorea: Cook's Bay
Moorea: Cook's Bay
Moorea: Cook's Bay
Moorea: Cook's Bay
Moorea: Cook's Bay
Moorea: Cook's Bay
Moorea: Cook's Bay from Air
Moorea: Cook's Bay from Air
Moorea: Cook's Bay from Air
Moorea: Cook's Bay from Air
Moorea: Cook's Bay from W. Moorea: Cook's Bay Mission
Moorea: Cook's Bay Opononu from Air
Moorea: Cook's Bay Opononu from Air
Moorea: Cook's Bay Opunohu from Air
Moorea: E Coast from Air
Moorea: E Coast from Air
Moorea: E from Air
Moorea: E from Air
Moorea: From Air
Moorea: From Mt.
Moorea: NE
Moorea: NE
Moorea: NE from Air
Moorea: NE from Air

Moorea: NE from Air
Moorea: NE. from Air
Moorea: Nth Coast from Air
Moorea: Opunoho
Moorea: Opunohu
Moorea: Opunohu
Moorea: Opunohu
Moorea: Opunohu
Moorea: Opunohu
Moorea: Opunohu
Moorea: Opunohu
Moorea: Opunohu
Moorea: Opunohu
Moorea: Opunohu
Moorea: Reef
Moorea: Sth From Air
Moorea: Sth Point from Air
Moorea: Sunset
Moorea: Sunset
Moorea: Sunset
Moorea: Sunset
Moorea: Sunset
Moorea: Sunset

HUAHINE
Huahine
Huahine
Huahine
Huahine Huahine
Huahine
Huahine
Huahine: From Raiatea

RAIATEA

Anthrop

Anthrop

Anthrop

Raiatea

Raiatea

Raiatea

Raiatea:

Raiatea: E Coast from Air

Raiatea: East

Raiatea: East

Raiatea: East

Raiatea: East

Raiatea: East

Raiatea: East

Raiatea: East

Raiatea: East

Raiatea: East

Raiatea: East

Raiatea: East Coast

Raiatea: East Coast

Raiatea: East Coast from Air

Raiatea: Faaroa

Raiatea: Faatiaapiti (Marae Tuputaauatea)

Raiatea: Fish in Lagoon

Raiatea: Fish in Lagoon

Raiatea: M. Taputapuatea

Raiatea: M. Taputapuatea

Raiatea: M. Taputapuatea

Raiatea: M. Taputapuatea

Raiatea: M. Taputapuatea

Raiatea: M. Taputapuatea

Raiatea: M. Taputapuatea

Raiatea: M. Taputapuatea

Raiatea: M. Taputapuatea

Raiatea: M. Taputapuatea
Raiatea: M. Taputapuatea
Raiatea: M. Taputapuatea
Raiatea: M. Taputapuatea
Raiatea: M. Taputapuatea
Raiatea: M. Taputapuatea
Raiatea: M. Taputapuatea
Raiatea: M. Taputapuatea (Tahaa)
Raiatea: Marae Tainuu
Raiatea: Marae Tainuu
Raiatea: Marae Tainuu
Raiatea: Marae Tainuu
Raiatea: Marae Tainuu
Raiatea: Motu Tetaro
Raiatea: Motu Tetaroi
Raiatea: Mt Orotaio
Raiatea: Mt Orotaio
Raiatea: Mt Orotaio
Raiatea: Opoa
Raiatea: Pass Teevaati from Air
Raiatea: Research Asst
Raiatea: Taputapuatea
Raiatea: Tohunaoe W. Coast
Raiatea: Tupua Bay Mt Orotaio
Raiatea: Utoroa
Raiatea: Uturoa
Raiatea: Uturoa from Air
Research Asst

BORA BORA
Bora Bora
Bora Bora: From Raiatea
Borabora: From Raiatea

TAHAA
Tahaa
Tahaa
Tahaa
Tahaa
Tahaa: From Raiatea
Tahaa: From Raiatea
Tahaa: From Raiatea
Tahaa: From Raiatea E

MANIHI
Manihi: Airport
Manihi: Airport
Manihi: Anthrop
Manihi: From Air
Manihi: Lagoon
Manihi: Res Asst
Manihi: Shore Line

HIVA OA
Atuona
Atuona
Atuona: Afternoon Sun
Atuona: Atikua
Atuona: Bay SE Copra Drier
Atuona: Beach
Atuona: Beach
Atuona: Beach & Valley
Atuona: Beach & Valley
Atuona: Bungalow & Chickens
Atuona: Bungalow Garden
Atuona: Dwellings on Old Paepae
Atuona: Gauguin's Grave
Atuona: Mt Temetiu
Atuona: Mt Temetiu

Atuona: Mt Temetiu from Cemetery
Atuona: Mt Temetiu: Rauzy's
Atuona: Paepae (Tohua?) Atikua
Atuona: Paepae Atikua
Atuona: Paepae Atikua
Atuona: Paepae Atikua Valley
Atuona: Paepae Maunaofefe
Atuona: Paepae Maunoa Fefe
Atuona: Paepae Maunoafefe
Atuona: Rauzy's Bungalow
Atuona: Rauzy's Bungalow
Atuona: Rauzy's Restaurant
Atuona: Tiki & Research Asst.
Atuona: Traitors' Bay Anakee Isle
Atuona: Traitors' Bay Pt Teaehoe
Atuona: Valley
Atuona: Vegetation Atikua
Atuona: Vegetation Atikua
Atuona: Vegetation Atikua
Atuona: Vegetation Atikua
Hiva Oa: Airport
Hiva Oa: Atuona from Air
Hiva Oa: Atuona Valley from Air
Hiva Oa: Atuona Valley from Air
Hiva Oa: Central Ridge E.
Hiva Oa: Coast East of Atuona
Hiva Oa: Fatuhiva & Anakee Isle
Hiva Oa: From Air
Hiva Oa: From Iva Iva
Hiva Oa: From Tekokuu
Hiva Oa: From Tekokuu
Hiva Oa: Hanaiapa
Hiva Oa: Hanapaba
Hiva Oa: NE Coast
Hiva Oa: NW Coast

Hiva Oa: NW Coast
Hiva Oa: NW Coast
Hiva Oa: Punaei & Tahuata
Hiva Oa: Rauzy & Airport
Hiva Oa: Ridge Nth of Airport
Hiva Oa: SE Coast
Hiva Oa: SE Coast
Hiva Oa: SW Coast from Air
Hiva Oa: SW Coast Mt Temuatua: Vaitepua
Hiva Oa: SW Coast Vaitepua
Hiva Oa: Taaoa
Hiva Oa: Taaoa
Hiva Oa: Taaoa
Hiva Oa: Taaoa
Hiva Oa: Taaoa
Hiva Oa: Taaoa
Hiva Oa: Taaoa
Hiva Oa: Traitors' Bay & Tahuata

TAHUATU
Tahuata
Tahuata: From Air
Tahuata: From Air
Tahuata: Hanamoenoa
Tahuata: Hanatefau & Hapatoni
Tahuata: Hanateyou
Tahuata: Hanene
Tahuata: Hapatoni
Tahuata: Iva Iva
Tahuata: Puniae
Tahuata: Uua Ridge
Tahuata: Uua Ridge from air
Tahuata: Vaitahu: Hapatoni: From Air
Tahuata: West Coast
Teiefitu Uma

Vaitahu

Vaitahu

Vaitahu: Children

Vaitahu: Children

Vaitahu: Children

Vaitahu: Children

Vaitahu: Children

Vaitahu: Children

Vaitahu: Children

Vaitahu: Children

Vaitahu: Children

Vaitahu: Children

Vaitahu: Children & Research Asst.

Vaitahu: Cove

Vaitahu: Cyprian

Vaitahu: From Air

Vaitahu: From Air

Vaitahu: From Air

Vaitahu: From Air

Vaitahu: From Air

Vaitahu: From Landing Place

Vaitahu: From Landing Place

Vaitahu: From Landing Place

Vaitahu: From Landing Place

Vaitahu: From North Path

Vaitahu: From Nth Path

Vaitahu: From Sth

Vaitahu: From Sth Path to Fort

Vaitahu: From Uma's House

Vaitahu: Hanamiai

Vaitahu: Hanamiai

Vaitahu: Hanamiai Bay

Vaitahu: Hanamiai Commune Boat: Taro's

Vaitahu: Hanamiai from Air

Vaitahu: Hanamiai Pass to Hapatoni

Vaitahu: Io's Cross
Vaitahu: Marie Ange
Vaitahu: Marie Ange
Vaitahu: Nth Point
Vaitahu: Nth Pt & Bay
Vaitahu: Nth Pt & Bay
Vaitahu: Old Paepae
Vaitahu: Old Paepae Present Dwellings
Vaitahu: Prot. Ch. Teinaei Paepae
Vaitahu: RC. Church Tohua Tootookokina
Vaitahu: St Point
Vaitahu: Tekeu
Vaitahu: Tekeu
Vaitahu: Tekeu from Nth Path
Vaitahu: Tekokuu
Vaitahu: The Expedition
Vaitahu: The Expedition
Vaitahu: Tohua Tootookokina
Vaitahu: Tohua Vahanekua
Vaitahu: Tohua Vahanekua
Vaitahu: Tohua Vahanekua
Vaitahu: Tohua Vahanekua
Vaitahu: Tohua Vahanekua
Vaitahu: Tohua Vahanekua
Vaitahu: Tohua Vahanekua
Vaitahu: Trail
Vaitahu: Trail
Vaitahu: Uua Ridge
Vaitahu: Uua Ridge
Vaitahu: Village Path

UA HUKA
Ua Huka
Ua Huka
Ua Huka

Ua Huka
Ua Huka
Ua Huka Ua Huka
Ua Huka
Ua Huka
Ua Huka
Ua Huka: Airport
Ua Huka: Airport

NUKUHIVA
Nukuhiva: E Coast
Nukuhiva: E. Coast
Nukuhiva: Hakaohoke
Nukuhiva: Hakapuuai
Nukuhiva: Hoo'umi
Nukuhiva: Mataua
Nukuhiva: mataua
Nukuhiva: Mataua Is
Nukuhiva: Sth Coast
Nukuhiva: Sth Coast
Nukuhiva: Sth Coast
Nukuhiva: Sth Coast
Nukuhiva: Sth Coast
Nukuhiva: SW Coast
Nukuhiva: Taipu & Hakapuuai
Nukuhiva: Tetokemaito
Nukuhiva: Tetokemaito
Nukuhiva: Tetokemaito Looking Nth
Taiohae
Taiohae
Taiohae
Taiohae: Admin: Beach
Taiohae: Anthrop on Pikivehine
Taiohae: Cathedral
Taiohae: East Arm

Taiohae: East Arm
Taiohae: East Arm
Taiohae: Fort Collet Pakiu
Taiohae: Hakapehi
Taiohae: Hauao Pakiu
Taiohae: N. Isle
Taiohae: NE Sector
Taiohae: NE Sector
Taiohae: NE Sector
Taiohae: NE Sector
Taiohae: Nth Sector
Taiohae: Nth Sector
Taiohae: Nth Sector
Taiohae: Nth Sector
Taiohae: Nth Sector
Taiohae: Nth Sector
Taiohae: Nth Sector
Taiohae: Nth Sector
Taiohae: Oata
Taiohae: Opening of Bay
Taiohae: Paepae Oata
Taiohae: Philomene's
Taiohae: Philomene's
Taiohae: Royal Tomb
Taiohae: Statue: Cathedral
Taiohae: Tiki
Taiohae: Tiki
Taiohae: Vaitu
Taiohae: Vegetation
Taiohae: Vegetation
Taiohae: Vegetation Oata
Taiohae: Vuhena
Taiohae: Vuhenua
Taiohae: W Arm
Taiohae: West Arm

www.ingramcontent.com/pod-product-compliance
Lightning Source LLC
Chambersburg PA
CBHW050809270326
41926CB00026B/4653